ONE MORE CHANCE

ONE MORE CHANCE

To End Nuclear Blackmail
Without Holocaust

DAYTON YOUNG

Exposition Press   New York

EXPOSITION PRESS, INC.

50 Jericho Turnpike, Jericho, New York 11753

FIRST EDITION

LIBRARY OF CONGRESS CATALOG CARD NUMBER: 72-90071

SBN 0-682-47609-9

To my grandchildren
and yours

Contents

*"Nothing is so powerful as an idea
whose time has come"*

Foreword and Summary

Certain widely unrecognized truths of the nuclear age are herein explored. These heretofore submerged truths are then correlated to show that the only type of world action which can reasonably be expected to end the horror of continuous nuclear *blackmail* has, at long last, suddenly become practical. But the evidence here presented also indicates that this current opportunity to salvage the future may be a very short-term opportunity —one which, if it is not grasped very quickly now, may be lost to humanity until *after* world holocaust has decimated and thoroughly humbled the human race.

The amiably conducted Nixon-Brezhnev summit meetings and the resulting understandings could conceivably lessen, at least temporarily, the danger of all-out nuclear war between the Americans and Russians. It was an admirable try. Likewise, the Nixon-Mao summit meetings were no doubt a step in the right direction and well deserved world applause. But, as these pages go to press, nothing in the current U.S. understandings with either Moscow or Peking seems likely to prevent rapid acceleration toward a final nuclear showdown *between Peking and Moscow*. And such a Moscow-Peking showdown could jeopardize the lives of hundreds of millions of "innocent bystanders." Of even more importance, none of these summit meetings or any of the other currently publicized proposals offers the slightest hope of ending the "over-all" game of nuclear *blackmail*. Every nation is automatically locked into that game as soon as it acquires a major nuclear arsenal. The reasons that none of the heretofore publicized agreements or proposals can hope to end nuclear blackmail will be fully examined elsewhere in these pages.

On his return from abroad on June 1, 1972, President Nixon correctly stated to the Congress that: "We bring back the *be-*

9

ginning of a process which could lead to a lasting peace. . . .
The threat of war has not been eliminated. . . . Never was
there a time when hope was more justified or *complacency more
dangerous."*

This book, then, is a detailed proposal for the desperately
needed *next* step in the process so auspiciously inaugurated by
Nixon's summit meetings.

Is any nation now anywhere near bluff-proof? Or is nuclear
blackmail indeed the central reality of daily life in the world's
leading nations? Can anyone who is well-informed seriously
doubt that if the U.S. were not "holding hostage" the key cities
and industries of the Soviet Union, the Kremlin long since
would have succeeded in forcing its own type of government on
most of the nations of Asia, Africa, and South America? Likewise, can there be any valid doubt that if Moscow were not
holding hostage the key cities and industries of the U.S., the
Americans long since would have stopped the Communist takeover of Cuba, the North Vietnamese invasion of South Vietnam,
and the like? Continuous nuclear blackmail is indeed central
to our daily lives.

But if (per evidence herein examined) nuclear blackmail
alone (*without* any actual launchings of nuclear missiles) can
turn large segments of the human race into pitiful psychopathic
cripples, why haven't the Russians and Americans *already* been
more severely crippled emotionally? The answer, of course, is
that (because both of the two present nuclear powers are highly
industrialized) they would stand to lose somewhat *equally* by a
"full nuclear exchange." For that reason, and also because both
Washington and Moscow are presently governed by thoughtful,
cool-headed officials, the danger of suddenly being burned alive
has been more theoretical than imminent. But as soon as nations
like Red China (whose leaders know they have far less to lose
by a full nuclear exchange) are ready to join in the nuclear
bluffing game, the emotional pressures (especially on the Russian
and Chinese peoples) will skyrocket. The evidence is clear that
no living creature can long continue to function normally when

it becomes aware that it faces sudden bodily destruction day and night, year after year, without hope of any "rest periods."

For the first time in all human history, great masses of people *are* now continuously exposed to the threat of suddenly being burned alive—a threat against which the individual can take no effective action—a threat that (per evidence herein) is unlikely to be alleviated by any of the plans of action now under consideration—a threat that will be enormously *intensified* as soon as Peking can reinforce with a few more nuclear weapons its *present* great strategic advantage, which is that it can far better *afford* the kind of losses both sides would suffer in a full nuclear exchange. Remember that Peking already has the world's third largest submarine fleet and is rapidly getting its key nuclear facilities deep underground.

Does Peking actually have sufficient motivation to risk losing its huge "surplus" population and what little *heavy* industry it may still have aboveground? Who was it that invented the phrase "go for broke"? Not only are the Chinese a very proud, stubborn, and fatalistic people, but they have an age-old tradition as "long-shot" gamblers. What would Peking have to *gain* by risking a nuclear showdown with Moscow? The 900,000 square miles of former Chinese territory now held by Moscow would not, alone, warrant the taking of such a risk. But add to that the chance for Peking to take over the world leadership of the "Communist" movement and, above all, the fact that many less bold and fatalistic peoples than the Chinese have not hesitated to risk "everything" to avoid "slavery" under a political system they considered wholly unsuited to their special needs. Whereas the Soviet system is controlled (at least allegedly) by the unpropertied *urban* worker, China's *basic* economy is agrarian. The difference is deep and great. But what about Moscow's recent offerings of "peaceful coexistence"? Who was it that *taught* the Peking regime never to believe a promise—that only fools keep promises that fail to yield them an advantage?

In short, Peking does have sufficient motivation to risk a final nuclear showdown with Moscow. At least, Moscow now appears to think so. And Peking is beginning to recognize that if it expects to save itself from a Moscow "takeover," it can't *wait* until the total of its weaponry equals that of Moscow. If Peking waits that long, its present great *strategic* advantage will be dissipated. Whereas a full nuclear exchange between Moscow and Peking three years hence would probably result in more *lasting* damage to the Russians than to the Chinese, the same probably would not be true a decade or so from now. By that time, Moscow might have its major targets *dispersed* all over the world, while Peking's most tempting targets would probably still be pretty well "bunched," as at present. So the logic of the situation seems to dictate that Peking either "goes for broke" in the next two to five years or resigns itself to "slavery" under the Russians.

For several years now, this writer has believed that the prospect of an early nuclear showdown between Peking and Moscow is sufficiently real that there is a good chance those two governments might now consider relinquishing their alleged necessity for world conquest *if* they could be shown a pattern of world organization that could fully protect all nations from each other. But only since the 1972 summit meetings has general awareness of this possibility been sufficient to warrant publication of this detailed proposal.

But what kind of world organization *could* conceivably end all nuclear blackmail and make every nation truly safe within its own borders? Could even a "world government" imposed by threat of force actually free the "home cities" of such a conqueror from the daily fear of mass cremation? No, it could not.

Eventually (if civilization is not destroyed meanwhile by actual nuclear war or by the emotional wreckage of continuous nuclear blackmail), the nations of the world will attain a sufficient degree of economic and cultural *parity* to make possible the setting up of a true world government by *voluntary* agreement. Such a voluntary world government might indeed be able to lift the cloud of panic fear from the human race. But to believe that such a time is anywhere near is to ignore all the lessons of history and the facts of "dirty old human nature."

Meanwhile, it should be obvious that a "takeover" by any full-fledged world government (whether controlled by Communists or by some group of international bankers) would *have* to involve the slaughter or violent oppression of tens or hundreds of millions of dissident individuals. And millions of survivors of such victims would feel fully motivated to risk their lives avenging their loved ones.

Just how would the ablest of these deeply wronged individuals go about destroying or holding hostage the home cities of such a conqueror? Would they need missiles, submarines, bombers, or other elaborate equpiment? Not if they were competent *smugglers*. Without an attempt in this Foreword to fully clinch the argument, it should be noted here that:

1. As stated by articles in various leading magazines, the 15 pounds or so of fissionable material needed to build a Hiroshima-type A-bomb could, even now, be stolen from most any of the atomic *power* plants that already ring the globe. The rapidly increasing number of these plants under various governments is rapidly *lessening* the possibility of preventing such theft. Alternatively, the fissionable material needed (by private individuals bent on blackmailing a world conqueror) could be hijacked in transit between governmental depots.

2. One of the top authorities on the building of A-bombs has repeatedly been quoted in the public print as saying: "I've been worried about how *easy* it is to build A-bombs ever since I first helped design them. . . . The whole job could be done in someone's basement with materials purchaseable anywhere. . . . All the once-secret data needed seeped into *un*classified literature long ago."

3. Even without any access to fissionable material, private individuals bent on wiping out the home-city populations of a brutal world conqueror could easily get the job done with a few bottles of plague germs or a few spoonfuls of water-supply poison.

4. Whereas no government with large cities and industries of its own to be held hostage can ever again make itself "bluff-proof," private individuals who had already lost everything they

held dear *would* be bluff-proof. No government anywhere has ever been able to stop all smuggling across its borders. And no government has ever been able to prevent the black marketeering of desperately wanted items (such as mass weapons components would be under a ruthless world conqueror).

5. If all the above is true, it may be asked why the Arab terrorists who held hostage and slaughtered the Olympic athletes did not, instead, hold the whole city of Tel Aviv hostage with a smuggled A-bomb. One answer might be that the Arab temperament has never been especially notable for the kind of cool efficiency and precision in long-range planning that would be necessary. But a better answer is that the undercover backers of the "Black September" terrorists knew world opinion would be *fully* consolidated against them if they slaughtered hundreds of thousands of Israeli civilians whose chief offense was that their government had won several small wars in which the Arabs themselves were the lawless aggressors.

By contrast with that situation, a group of terrorists who destroyed or held hostage the home cities of a ruthless world conqueror (to paralyze the World Government imposed by such conqueror), would probably have the strong (though unspoken), moral support of most of the nations being ground under such conqueror's heel.

The frequent hijacking of airliners can be stopped because an airliner is comparatively easy to guard against smugglers of bombs and other weapons. But the hijacking of a world conqueror's home cities could not be stopped. No government could long afford the "solid wall" of armed guards that would be needed night and day around the entire perimeter of each great city. So the city or cities from which any brutal world conquest *emanated* would probably be wiped out even before such conquest was fully completed—and long before such conqueror's World Government could fully stabilize its control. No matter how often the conqueror's governing bureaucracy was replaced or relocated, the remaining key cities of the conqueror's homeland would never have any respite from the gut-searing terror of imminent cremation. And whereas the passengers on a hijacked airliner seldom become insane (because they are kept in a state of wild alarm for only a few hours or few days), the millions of residents of a world conqueror's home cities could be kept in a state of wild alarm night and day, year after year, until such unrelenting emotional pressure drove most of them stark mad.

No, a forcibly-imposed world government is *not* the solution to the problem of ending the daily threat of mass cremation.

It should be pointed out without delay, however, that *national or local* governments are never likely to be at the mercy of such private individuals armed with mass weapons. Whereas perfectly sane and very capable men could bring themselves to wipe out the home cities of a brutal conqueror, the kind of crackpot who might consider wiping out millions of his *own* countrymen just wouldn't "have what it takes" to organize the teamwork and logistics of a personal atomic war.

But if no national or even world government (having large cities and industries of its own to be held hostage) can hope to make itself bluff-proof and immune to sudden cremation, what is left to consider? Could a nuclear-armed United Nations police force be made bluff-proof and capable of carrying out its charter obligations? Most certainly it could not. The huge staff of non-military diplomats, their families, their clerical staffs, and the whole city of New York would inevitably be held hostage to render any such force impotent. Furthermore, the basic principles of political control on which the U.N. charter was based are such that (even if the U.N. *could* be made bluff-proof militarily) it could never be trusted with invulnerable military power. It could never be acceptably safeguarded against subversion and takeover without completely scrapping its present charter and functions.

But if a nuclear-armed international police force had no non-military possessions or personnel that could successfully be held hostage and if all its expendable personnel and weapons were dispersed underseas and among tiny remote islets around the globe, such an agency *could* be made fully bluff-proof and fully capable of enforcing a certain type of anti-aggression laws.

The big remaining problem, then, would be to adequately safe-guard such an agency from subversion and takeover. This is *not* impossible. Given the type of charter herein roughly blueprinted, a nuclear-armed international police force *could be made less of a risk for every nation than every nation must hereafter face without such a protector.*

For easy reference, the special kind of bluff-proof and ade-quately subversion-proof international police force here proposed will be called a "UNAFORCE." Its charter would give it no responsibility or authority to interfere in the domestic affairs of any nation. Nor would its charter give to Unaforce personnel any major decision-making powers. Because recent developments make it feasible, at last, to incorporate in a Unaforce charter a set of enforceable *boundary lines* for each nation, all major de-cisions regarding imposition of penalties could be made *for* the Unaforce staff either by the wording of the charter itself or by the type of "World Emergency Court" herein outlined. The security and integrity of such a court could be adequately safe-guarded by much the same principles and devices proposed for Unaforce itself.

With the type of charter here proposed, a Unaforce could not greatly wrong any nation except by actually *violating* its own charter. And any violation of the Unaforce charter would instantly lose for every nation the only real security from foreign attack that it had ever known or could ever hope to know. The only nations that would ever *want* Unaforce to violate its charter would be ones bent on *world conquest* against utterly impossible odds. Since the type of charter here proposed would make it practically impossible for more than ⅓ of Unaforce personnel to be influenced by a potential world conqueror, the odds against charter violation would be astronomical. For a long list of good reasons herein supplied, this Unaforce would be even *less* vul-nerable to subversion and takeover than was the U.S. military establishment when *that* body held a world monopoly of the new mass weapons.

In attempting to present a proposal with such unlimited ramifications, it is of course impossible to outguess the reader as to which objections most deserve earliest consideration. But as the answer (or at least *an* answer) to your "pet" objection is doubtless included somewhere in these pages, please be a little patient.

If any of the "recognized experts" were actually valid authorities on how to prevent the escalation of the nuclear blackmail horror, there would be no need for this unknown to "get into the act." But since there *are* no valid authorities to whom we can turn for "guaranteed" solutions of the world's one most pressing problem, all thinking men will do well to assess the logic here presented. Before giving up hope (or relaxing into the complacency that President Nixon says is our greatest danger), even the busiest of men can surely afford to risk enough of their time to reach an *informed* judgment on the only proposal for ending nuclear blackmail that has not *yet* been proved impractical.

Just where, by the way, would Red China fit into the Unaforce pattern? Right now (even if the Peking regime were short-sighted enough to want to), Peking could not prevent the setting up and implementing of the kind of Unaforce here proposed. And, once in operation, such a Unaforce could not avoid giving to the Chinese precisely the same security from all interference in their domestic affairs as it would provide to every other nation. But failure to act quickly now on this proposal might well enable Peking to block its adoption.

Is it unrealistic and Utopian to hope that the Soviet Union, the U.S., and their respective allies can now be interested in cooperating to set up a Unaforce? From 1945 until very recent months, that would indeed have been a Utopian dream. Throughout those years, the U.S. and the Soviet Union were taking turns at feeling temporarily secure without any "outside" help. But this proposal is *no longer* premature. It is finally beginning to dawn on the Russians as well as the Americans that nothing they can hope to do by and for themselves can ever end the growing threat to any viable civilization.

Would even the *U.S.* now be willing to risk the establishment of any fully bluff-proof international agency? Don't ever forget that, way back when the present U.N. charter was being formulated and when the U.S. had no immediate *need* of a fully bluff-proof protector, *the U.S. did actually offer to negotiate for the atomic arming of an international enforcement agency.* That offer did not *then* appeal to the Kremlin because it knew perfectly well that it would be in no danger of an unprovoked attack by the only atomic power then in sight. But with the Chinese now rapidly acquiring great nuclear power, it is entirely reasonable to expect that any such offer as the U.S. made in the 1940s (to negotiate the creation of a fully bluff-proof antiaggression agency) would now be of very great interest to the Russians—as the only feasible *alternative* to a disastrous nuclear showdown between them and the Chinese.

Now that we have had a quick birds-eye view of the "forest," let's get on with a closer examination of the individual "trees"— to see if they could collectively withstand the hurricanes of human passion. No X-ray will be needed to spot a few trees that need treatment by competent specialists. No virgin forest ever consisted of all *perfect* trees. But at a time when none of the *other* forests in sight can hope to shelter us from the coming storm, this one surely warrants the best efforts of the best specialists available.

WHY THE ODD FORMAT OF THIS BOOK?

It consists of (1) a Foreword that amounts to a short summary, (2) an *expanded* summary of 15 fundamental truths, which follows *this* page, (3) a Unaforce organization chart, and (4) the main body of the tentatively suggested provisions for a Unaforce charter, under the heading, "Question and Answer Appendix."

It will be obvious that these different segments were written at widely different times—from 1945 to 1972, in fact. And if the nature of the subject matter had not now suddenly become so desperately urgent, a comprehensive revision of the format might now be warranted. Such a revision might consolidate in one place every one of the arguments offered in support of each phase of the proposal. On the other hand, such a "bunching" behind each controversial statement of *all* the detail needed to fully support it would undoubtedly cause many readers to lose perspective and interest while "wading through" detail that might seem irrelevant to their pet criticisms. There simply is no sure way to make so complex a problem and proposal both fully convincing and fully assimilable at a quick glance. But stay with it. An answer to *your* chief criticism is almost certainly to be found somewhere herein.

ONE MORE CHANCE

The 15 Widely Ignored Truths Which Invalidate Every Alternative

to This Proposal

Because world leaders are still trying to dodge certain truths (as herein printed in capital leters), the one kind of approach that now seems to offer real hope of averting world catastrophe is being neglected. Turning our backs on these truths cannot make them go away or prevent them from destroying us. But it is not surprising that those who must bear the chief responsibility for the world's fate do not publicly acknowledge truths that, when taken *separately,* seem to contain no element of hope. And it is probable that such truths never will be faced publicly by politicians until they can be fitted into some pattern of action that does offer reasonable grounds for hope.

This book is an attempt to focus the attention of world leaders on a pattern of world organization that does contain the seeds of valid hope because it is *not* incompatible with the "submerged" truths of the nuclear age. Of course any peace proposal that, like this one, is without historical precedent is unlikely to get serious consideration unless and until at least Washington and Moscow can be shown that none of the *alternative* plans of action can protect their most vital interests. Therefore one of the primary purposes of these pages is to demonstrate just *why* none of the alternatives available (to less-than-Godlike humans) has any reasonable chance of preventing the early escalation of the nuclear blackmail threat to human sanity.

To get on, then, with our 15 heretofore submerged truths of the nuclear age, the first, and one of the more obvious, is that:

I. NO "GOVERNMENT," AS SUCH, CAN EVER AGAIN,

23

BY ITS *OWN* EFFORTS, MAKE ITSELF BLUFF-PROOF
AND THEREBY FREE ITS PEOPLE OF THE CONTIN-
UOUS THREAT OF SUDDEN ANNIHILATION. NOR
CAN ANY COALITION OF JUST A FEW GOVERN-
MENTS HOPE TO DO SO.

The non-military assets (cities, industries and the like) of
any full-fledged government are the natural targets for the new
weapons of mass destruction. No matter how heavily armed
such a possessor of non-military targets may be, those targets can
always be held hostage by a sufficiently reckless nuclear blackmailer to bluff that government into yielding a few points or the
whole game. For instance, during the past decade, neither of the
world's two most heavily armed goverments has been anywhere
near bluff-proof, not for one day or one hour. But up to now,
the danger of an actual nuclear exchange has not been very
great because the U.S. and the U.S.S.R. could have damaged
each other almost *equally* in such an exchange. However, when
nations having much less to lose in a nuclear exchange get
themselves in position to make a surprise nuclear attack (perhaps
as little as two or three years hence), the lack of any fully bluff-
proof authority in the world may spell real disaster for all.

In the ages before the advent of mass weapons, such posses-
sors of nonmilitary targets as the Roman Empire or England
could, by their own efforts, feel secure from successful attack
for decades at a time. But now that a nuclear attacker can have
even a faint hope of "winning" an unannounced war in minutes,
no government (handicapped by its possession of non-military
targets) can ever again do anything by and for itself (or with
the help of comparably handicapped allies) that could make it
bluff-proof against a reckless nuclear blackmailer. Nothing that
Moscow, for instance, can hope to do by and for itself, can end
the daily threat of nuclear attack by Peking.

So what? Mankind is a very tough breed. Is there any real
evidence that great masses of people may develop a strangling
mass psychosis just because (for the first time in human history),
the threat of being burned alive is now *continuous and growing*,
rather than intermittent?

Researchers working with various kinds of animals (both caged and in their native habitats) have found that complete nervous breakdown or death can be induced in the test animals by making them aware they are in continuous danger of bodily injury night and day with no prospect of relief. For instance a recent three-year study by the Missouri Department of Conservation may shed some light on the question. That organization had long been puzzled by the large numbers of very *young* cottontail rabbits found dead in the fields with no visible evidence of starvation, predators' teeth, or gunshot wounds. Whereas in the security of captivity, such animals have a life expectancy of around five years, most of those found dead without a scratch on them were not over *one* year old. Of what did they die? Thousands of post-mortems conducted by the Missouri Department of Conservation showed that death was due, in most cases, to *stomach ulcers or hypertension* resulting from overstimulated adrenal glands. In other words, they had been "frightened to death" because they could find no safe place to hide from their enemies for even a few hours at a time. If wild rabbits live only one fifth of their normal lifespan when continuously deprived of all bodily security, may not great masses of humans be incapacitated in their teens if continuously exposed to a sharp escalation of that intolerable stress?

Are the emotional problems of tough old mankind at all comparable to those of the timid rabbit? Well, let's see. Don't even the bravest of human *soldiers* have to be hospitalized with "battle-fatigue" if kept directly in the front line of battle for too many months without any "secure" rest-periods? But *you* (Bob, Ivan, Ching, Olaf, Tojo, Guiseppe) have all been continuously in the "front-line trenches" for years now. And your psyches (especially those of your young) are beginning to show the strain. Somewhere in our subconscious, each of us knows that there is never a moment's respite from the threat of surprise attack—not the old type of attack for which a people could prepare themselves while their border guards *delayed* the enemy's advance. Nuclear blackmail is a *direct* threat to the person of every civilian, an *ever-present* threat of personal bodily harm.

Unless something is done soon to end that continuous threat to the lives of helpless civilians, millions of them will "come unstuck" from "battle-fatigue." Fear is tolerable—even needed—by rabbits, tigers, and men—up to a point. But the *continuous* fear that the body may be torn apart or burned without warning at any moment will destroy any species emotionally.

Some stoics feel the nuclear threat (like the age-old threat of earthquake, hurricane, and flood) has become a "constant" with which the world can learn to live—that after an eventual nuclear holocaust life will, in due time, "go on much as before." To be sure, even if several hundred million of the world's "surplus population" were suddenly cremated tomorrow a single such event might not end all civilization. After all, instant extermination of such millions might be a more "merciful" solution of the overpopulation problem than their slow starvation would be. But an immediate one-time wipeout of a few hundred million lives is *not* the greatest danger the world faces in the nuclear age. A far greater threat to all human progress is the fact that continuous exposure over a period of years to a sharply increasing level of emotional pressure can render most citizens of the major nations wholly incapable of constructive thought and action. Great "natural" disasters sometimes kill a few thousand people but they never produce millions of psychopathic cripples. The citizens of major nations can *not* "learn to live with" greatly intensified and continuous nuclear blackmail as they have long ago learned to live with occasional earthquake and floods. Although soldiers hospitalized with "battle-fatigue" often regain their sanity, they can *not* do so while remaining exposed to the "front-line pressures" which caused their collapse. What then is being proposed by world leaders that could possibly insulate civilians from the fast-rising "front-line pressures" of nuclear blackmail?

Even today, many severe cases of "urban anxiety" being treated by psychiatrists are doubtless due more to subconscious fear of urban cremation than to traffic jams, pollution, street crime, or job insecurity. In Russia, the great interest in their new "electrosleep" machine cannot all be attributed to the bad wheat crop or to the friendly neighborhood secret police. The recent sharp increase in acute insomnia among the more advanced peoples can hardly be blamed on the old prenuclear type of worries. But, up to now, perhaps the most serious impact of nuclear blackmail on human effectiveness can be seen in the growing epidemic (especially among highly sensitized intellectuals) of what psychiatrists are calling "divorcement from reality." What are the symptoms? The press and airways daily carry pronouncements by formerly respected thinkers who obviously now have a type of emotional "block" that enables them to *ignore* blandly many of the most significant facts of human history stored somewhere in their brains. Why, after all the millennia of human frustration, has this disastrous malady only recently become noteworthy? If this disastrous type of "mental block" were primarily the result of prenuclear types of emotional pressure, why wasn't it of epidemic proportions back in prenuclear days?

Is fear-bread hysteria now affecting the older generation as much as it is the world's youth? Certainly not. The generation which now rules the world has foolishly (and selfishly) imagined that the real disaster can be postponed until they *personally* are "well out of it." But the young are beginning to know by blind instinct that such cowardly postponement cannot help *them*. They know instinctively that failure of their elders to face the new truths of the nuclear age immediately will turn what should be the best years of their lives into years of intolerable horror.

And the growing hysteria of intellectual youth is even more evident in many parts of the Communist world than in the "Free World." Only in Russia, perhaps, is youthful hysteria less in evidence right now, because Russian youth has been deluded into hoping that it will soon be in command of a World Government capable of *suppressing* all threats to itself and its home cities. *Could* a World Government imposed by brute force (or the threat thereof) ever hope to free itself and its home cities from daily fear of sudden annihilation? Before answering that question (with the second of our fourteen or more neglected truths), let us first concede that a true World Government, voluntarily agreed on by all nations, is eventually inevitable and that such a *voluntary* association of the nations would have an excellent chance of ending humanity's present reign of terror. As all nations gradually become mechanized, automated, computerized, and tuned in on the *same* worldwide broadcasts, they will, of necessity, all move in the direction now being taken by the member-nations of the European Common Market. It has been possible to create the Common Market in our time *only* because each of the member nations *already* shares much the same type of culture and much the same level of economic development. By contrast, any world government formed in the next few decades would have to *force* a considerable proportion of the world's people into a straight jacket for which they are nowhere near ready—and which they would fight to the death.

Of course the so-called Communist regimes have no illusion that they can put all the world under one government in the next few decades *except* by human slaughter on a vast scale. And it is hard to believe that an international-banker clique (and its affiliated academic groups in the free world) who are alleged by Carrol Quigley, to be financing world revolution with a view to setting up a world dictatorship of their own, could be ignorant enough of basic human nature to believe they could soon set up such a world dictatorship without massive bloodshed. In short, the idea that any full-fledged world government could be set up in the next couple of decades without vast human slaughter seems too unreal to need serious rebuttal. So, during the decades while the world's nations are maturing enough to permit *voluntary* formation of a true world government, some interim pattern is desperately needed to avert a daily threat of mass annihilation, because no *forcibly* imposed world government can hope to do so. Why? Because:

II. EVEN A *WORLD* GOVERNMENT (IF ESTABLISHED BY FORCE OR THREAT OF FORCE), WOULD ALWAYS BE AT THE MERCY OF DEEPLY WRONGED PRIVATE *INDIVIDUALS* WHO COULD SUCCESS-

FULLY BLACKMAIL IT WITH MASS WEAPONS, THE
COMPONENTS OF WHICH THEY HAD STOLEN AND
SMUGGLED INTO THE CONQUEROR'S HOME CITIES.

A world government that did *not* have control over the daily
lives and property of its citizens would be of no value to the conqueror who had set it up. One which *did* exercise such control
could never be free of the threat of sudden mass annihilation. Its
home cities would continually be held hostage by some of the
millions of individuals whose loved ones had been liquidated or
tortured by the conqueror, and such individuals would be
virtually bluff-proof. When a government (a possessor of large
cities and industries) is threatened by another government (one
possessing similarly vulnerable targets for mass weapons), the
two have *some* chance of bluffing each other to a standstill. But
how could a conqueror's world government go about bluffing out
possessionless private *individuals* who felt they had nothing left
to live for but revenge? Such individuals would *need* no complex
missiles, submarines, or bombers to destroy any group of cities in
the world. Nothing could prevent some of them from stealing the
simple components of crude A-bombs (or a few bottles of plague
germs or water-supply poison) and *smuggling* this devastation
into the conqueror's home cities. Is this an unrealistic fantasy?

As spelled out by the May 1969 issue of *U.S. News and
World Report,* the fifteen pounds or so of fissionable material
needed to build a Hiroshima-type A-bomb could be stolen from
some of the many atomic *power* plants that now ring the globe.
Or they might be hijacked in transit from one to another of the
weapons depots of various governments. Furthermore, one of
the world's top nuclear authorities is quoted as saying: "I've
been worried about how easy it is to build A-bombs ever since I
first helped design them. The whole job could be done in someone's basement with materials purchaseable anywhere. Once a
criminal group succeeded in getting the (fissionable materials)
needed to make a bomb-mass 'critical,' they would have almost
no trouble putting it together into a weapon. All the once-secret
data needed to build bombs like those dropped on Japan seeped
into *un*classified literature long ago."

Could a world-conqueror's secret police infallibly detect all thieves and smugglers? Such police would probably force all citizens to spy on their friends and train all children to betray their parents. How could a smuggler of small packages containing A-bomb components hope to escape such a network? Well, how did Lenin and Trotsky so easily and often slip past all the Czar's brutal secret police? How then could any forcibly imposed world government hope to defend itself and its home cities from the bluff-proof survivors of its bloody purges?

Does this mean that *national* governments are in great danger from *individual* smugglers of mass weapons? Probably not. Whereas many citizens of brutally conquered countries might feel justified in destroying the conqueror's home cities, they would hardly be inclined to wipe out millions of their *own* fellow-countrymen—unless they were badly unbalanced emotionally. And such "crackpots" just wouldn't "have what it takes" to organize the logistics of stealing, smuggling, assembling, and hiding atomic weapons. But any government which relies on torture and liquidation of dissenters to take over the world must certainly expect to be at the mercy of tens of thousands of perfectly sane and competent relatives of its victims—each with entirely adequate motivation for risking his life. In short, the idea of a World Government established by ruthless force has been rendered wholly impractical by the fact that the new mass weapons cannot much longer be kept out of the hands of black-marketeers and individual smugglers.

III. EVEN IF THE UNITED NATIONS CHARTER WERE SUCH THAT THE U.N. COULD BE *TRUSTED* WITH NUCLEAR WEAPONS, IT STILL COULD NOT SUCCESSFULLY ENFORCE INTERNATIONAL ANTI-AGGRESSION LAWS, BECAUSE IT WOULD STILL NOT BE ANYWHERE NEAR BLUFF-PROOF.

The U.N. is definitely needed as it now is—for continuous communication between all nations. But in order for it to perform its present function as a continuous "debating society," the U.N. must have a large staff of *resident* diplomats, their families, office staffs, and so on. All these civilians naturally consider themselves "non-expendable," and they would make fine hostages for any nuclear aggressor. Regardless of the size of its armament, the U.N.'s decision-makers, together with their families and the whole city of New York could always be held hostage by a reckless aggressor to blackmail the U.N. into inaction.

IV. THE ONLY KIND OF WORLD ENTITY THAT *CAN* BE MADE BLUFF-PROOF IN THE NEXT FEW DECADES (AND THEREFORE CAPABLE OF PREVENTING AN EARLY NUCLEAR SHOWDOWN BETWEEN PEKING AND MOSCOW) WILL BE ONE THAT DOES *NOT* CONTROL OR LAY CLAIM TO ANY CIVILIAN POPULATIONS, CITIES, OR LARGE INDUSTRIES. SUCH A PURELY MILITARY OR POLICE AGENCY (WITH ITS OWN NUCLEAR SUBMARINES BASED ON TINY, REMOTE ISLETS ALL AROUND THE GLOBE) CAN INDEED BE MADE INVULNERABLE TO SUCCESSFUL ATTACKS AND THEREFORE BLUFF-PROOF.

But before examining some of the principles needed to make a militarily invulnerable "WORLD ANTI-AGGRESSION ENFORCEMENT AGENCY" ACCEPTABLY secure from takeover and misuse, let's give such an agency a handier name. A precise acronym would be "Wanaforce," but perhaps the name "UNAFORCE" would have a more general appeal. Also, before getting into the problem of safeguarding a Unaforce from subversion and takeover, let's briefly examine the chances of getting a charter for such a Unaforce actually adopted. Is there, for instance, any good reason to believe that the Soviet Union might now, at long last, be shown the selfish advantage to themselves in such a program? Consider that:

V. UNLESS MOSCOW AND PEKING CAN BE FULLY PROTECTED FROM EACH OTHER BY SOME FORCE BEYOND THE CONTROL OF EITHER, AN EARLY

SHOWDOWN BETWEEN THEM FOR THE LEADER-
SHIP OF THE "WORLD-CONQUEST MOVEMENT"
IS INEVITABLE.

The goal of world-conquest for which both Moscow and
Peking have already sacrificed scores of millions of their own
people's lives is an *indivisible* goal. Even if it were possible for
the two regimes to agree amicably on a division of world-control
between them, such an arrangement could not give either of
them any more security from nuclear threats than they now have
—which is none at all. Each one's mass targets would forever be
held hostage by the nuclear weapons of the other. Nor will it be
possible for the Russian and Chinese regimes to merge their
vastly divergent needs and aims into *one* homogeneous world
leadership, unless one cravenly submits to the will of the other.
But the needs and aims of the two peoples are essentially irreconcilable, and Peking has made it *very* clear that it considers *no*
price too high to pay for avoiding submission to Moscow's will.
Even a year or so ago, when Peking had almost *no* nuclear
weapons, it did not hesitate to attack Soviet border guards,
thereby risking sudden annihilation by the world's greatest
nuclear power. When an almost unarmed Peking feels it has
enough *strategic* advantage to risk a nuclear showdown (as it has
repeatedly done with both the Soviet and U.S. powers), why
should anyone imagine that Peking will "knuckle under" to
Moscow a few years hence when Peking will have greatly
expanded nuclear armaments?

Does Peking actually have sufficient motivation to risk all in
an eventual showdown with Moscow? Don't forget that Moscow
refuses to give back nearly a million square miles of territory
long claimed by Peking. The resulting "loss of face" to the very
face-conscious Chinese is a heavy handicap to Peking in its drive
to gain new adherents among uncommitted nations—new adherents it desperately needs if it is ever to realize its dream of
escaping Moscow's domination. To the proud, stubborn, fatalistic,
kamikaze types in Peking, the prospect of a Chinese bloodletting
sufficient to conquer many occidental peoples is unlikely to be a
deterrent. Of what does Peking's great *strategic* advantage

consist? Also, if Moscow's and Peking's interests are truly irreconcilable, why is Moscow now suddenly trying to create an illusion of growing harmony between them?

VI. RIGHT NOW (IN ANY SHOWDOWN FOR THE LEADERSHIP OF WORLD "COMMUNISM"), THE ODDS ARE TEMPORARILY IN MOSCOW'S FAVOR. BUT UNLESS MOSCOW CAN FORCE A FINAL SHOWDOWN *BEFORE* PEKING IS READY (PERHAPS 3 YEARS HENCE), THE *STRATEGIC* ODDS WILL, FOR A SHORT TIME, SWITCH TO PEKING. THEN, UNLESS PEKING TAKES PROMPT ADVANTAGE OF ITS *TEMPORARILY* FAVORABLE ODDS, THE STRATEGIC ADVANTAGE MAY GRADUALLY SWING BACK TO MOSCOW—LEAVING PEKING COMPLETELY AT MOSCOW'S MERCY. THESE CIRCUMSTANCES DICTATE A CONCLUSIVE MOSCOW-PEKING SHOWDOWN WITHIN 2 TO 5 YEARS—LONG *BEFORE* MOSCOW COULD "SAFELY" ISSUE ITS FINAL ULTIMATUM TO THE U.S. IF MOSCOW WERE TO TRY TO "BEAT PEKING'S TIMETABLE" BY AN EARLY SURPRISE ATTACK ON THE U.S., RUSSIAN LOSSES WOULD LEAVE MOSCOW *COMPLETELY* AT PEKING'S MERCY.

In attempting to justify this complex prophecy, we need to face an irrefutable truth, as follows:

VII. THAT NATION WHICH BELIEVES IT CAN BEST AFFORD TO LOSE WHAT IT WOULD BE *SURE* TO LOSE BY A MAJOR NUCLEAR EXCHANGE WILL ALWAYS HAVE THE UPPER HAND IN ANY NUCLEAR BLUFFING GAME.

Right now, while Peking does not have enough mass weapons to destroy any very major part of the Soviet potential (by even a surprise attack), Moscow feels it can "better afford" a nuclear exchange than can Peking. Therefore the odds are still in

Moscow's favor. But as soon as Peking could hope (by a surprise attack) to destroy even 20% of the Soviet potential, then Peking will have the upper hand in their nuclear bluffing game—even though Moscow's submarines and other weapons could still wipe out half or two thirds of the Chinese population, because:

(a) Whereas the rebuilding of even 20% of Moscow's vast industrial complexes would take many years, the Chinese economy is geared to little "cottage industries," which could be functioning again almost as soon as the ground cooled off.

(b) Whereas the Soviet Union has not fully recovered from its World War II manpower drain and cannot afford the loss of even 20% of its inadequate work force, Peking has an enormous *surplus* of manpower and undoubtedly feels it could afford to risk losing half or more of its total population for a chance to gain world domination.

So Peking undoubtedly feels if it is to escape complete subservience to Moscow it must force a showdown for the Communist leadership during the brief interval after it has the modest nuclear arsenal needed to give it the *strategic* upper hand —and *before* Moscow can fully consolidate its gains in the Near East, the Caribbean, South America, Southeast Asia, and elsewhere.

But let's go over that once more. It's a vital point. Whether or not the Kremlin would consider working with the U.S. to set up a bluff-proof Unaforce depends to a considerable extent on what chance it *thinks* it has of making itself bluff-proof *without* a Unaforce. With China rapidly gaining in nuclear strength, it is obvious that, ten or fifteen years hence, the only way the Kremlin could hope to be even a little bit bluff-proof would be by dispersing its weaponry (and part of its industrial strength) to remote corners of the globe while Peking's total potential remains largely concentrated in one neat "target-package." Since Peking must be keenly aware that it is making no noticeable progress toward dispersing its weapons and assets all over the globe—while Moscow is making very rapid strides in that direction—Peking can't help recognizing that 10 or 15 years hence the odds against Chinese supremacy are likely to be far greater than they will be two or three years hence. So if Peking is to avoid complete subservience to Moscow, it must force the final showdown *before* Moscow can get itself fully entrenched in the Mideast, India, South America, Africa, and so on. Moscow knows that Peking recognizes the elements of the situation and that Peking is therefore very apt to risk a final showdown for the Communist leadership in the next five years or less. Because Moscow does already have at least some comprehension of the situation, it *should* be fairly easy to show Moscow that the setting-up of a fully bluff-proof Unaforce is a subject worthy of immediate discussion and negotiation while there is yet time.

Why then is Moscow now attempting to create an illusion of growing harmony between itself and Peking? Because (in lieu of a fully bluff-proof agency to protect all nations from each other) Moscow has no *other* option as viable as pretended harmony. Is it really possible that today's greatest nuclear power is all that hard up for viable alternatives? Let's take a close look at each one of the Kremlin's options for dealing with the Chinese threat.

A. An immediate surprise nuclear strike by Moscow against Red China.

This "preemptive strike" option may currently have the most appeal to the Kremlin, but it probably could not maintain the power of the Kremlin at even its present level. Why? Because:

1. Although Peking probably does not *yet* have enough extreme-range nuclear missiles, bombers, or submarines to make an impressive counterattack, such elaborate equipment might not be *necessary* for a devastating Chinese counterattack. It is not unreasonable to assume that the astute Chinese may already have *smuggled* into Russian target areas chemical or biological weapons or the components of crude atom bombs—to be used only if and when Moscow makes a surprise nuclear attack. Could not the Soviet secret police armed with detection devices such as geiger-counters reliably locate and remove any such smuggled threats to the Kremlin's security? If you were a resident of any Russian key city, would you care to bet your life on that

possibility? How many times in a *decade* could a technically trained and equipped police force test each of the more than five billion acres of the Soviet Union to detect the presence of 15-pound lots of fissionable material? And what kind of scientific instrument could detect a bottle of botulin poison (sufficient to destroy the whole population of a great city when it is dumped into the public water supply) if such bottles already lie buried (by China's agents) in Russian key cities?

In short, it may *already* be too late for the Kremlin to improve its present precarious position by a surprise attack on the Chinese. Without a truly bluff-proof Unaforce to protect *all* nations from each other, the Kremlin's only real chance of regaining the *strategic* upper hand in its blackmail game with Peking probably lies in the Kremlin's chance of effecting a world-wide *dispersal* of its key people and its major industrial targets (as well as of its weapons) before Peking can effect a comparable dispersal. Don't ever forget that a nuclear blackmailer (like a plane hijacker) can "win" the game only if his opponent can be *bluffed* out. If the threatener is actually forced to *carry out* his threat, neither side actually wins. In the absence of a fully bluff-proof Unaforce having no blackmailable targets of its own, the "winner" of the Moscow-Peking struggle for supremacy will probably be that nation that sincerely *believes* it has the least to *lose* by a nuclear exchange. And Peking is almost certainly that one. If that is true, Moscow would indeed be wise to lose no time discussing with the U.S. the security-potential of a Unaforce.

2. There is yet another potential reason that may prove valid. At least some prominent nuclear scientists now believe (as a result of years of computer studies of infant and fetal mortality rates in areas downwind from the sites of past atomic and nuclear tests) that although the fallout from such tests did not seem to cause the death of adults, such fallout did sharply increase the death rate among babies in the womb and up to one year old. The conclusion reached by that group of investigators was that any nation launching a full-scale nuclear attack would thereby destroy *most* of the entire world's baby crop, even if such attacks were not followed by *any* counter-attack. Whether

or not nuclear fallout is actually that much more fatal to babies than to adults has not been proven to the satisfaction of many other scientists. But if the Kremlin should become convinced that the Sternglass theory can be substantiated, that reason *alone* might suffice to keep them from launching a preemptive strike against China. Peking doubtless feels it can far better afford to lose its entire baby-crop than can the Soviet Union, which is still suffering an acute manpower shortage. The prospect of losing its whole baby-crop (as well as a hundred million or so of its adults) is unlikely to prevent Peking from forcing a nuclear showdown with Moscow as soon as it feels it has the *strategic* upper hand, perhaps 3 years hence.

In any case, the option of a *preemptive* nuclear strike by Moscow against Peking is *not* a viable option. In the long run, Moscow would probably come out on the short end of such a proceeding, because (as more fully spelled out elsewhere in these pages) the highly industrialized Russians could not *recover* so quickly and fully from a nuclear exchange as could the little "cottage industries" in badly overpopulated China.

B. What about Moscow's option of entering into a "mutual aid pact" with the U. S. against Red China? Is that a viable option?

Even the naive and often-deceived Americans would not be stupid enough to enter into such a pact with a government that (after World War II) promptly betrayed its allies by launching a massive attempt to "destroy them from within." Any such mutual aid pact between Washington and Moscow would serve only to protect the Kremlin *while* it was gaining domination of enough more of the world to feel safe *without* U.S. support against Peking. By entering into such a pact with Moscow against Peking (and honoring it for long), the U.S. would be inviting its own doom. All the while the Americans were helping to keep the Chinese off the Russians' backs, Moscow would be so strongly entrenching itself in every continent that it would eventually feel "safe enough" in issuing a final ultimatum to the U.S. Even assuming that the Kremlin could eventually increase its indirect manipulation of many U.S. newsmen enough to get a Washington-Moscow mutual aid pact signed, there is simply *no* chance that it could pull off such a coup *before* Peking is ready for its final showdown with the Russians.

C. Could a three-way "arms limitation agreement" (among Washington, Moscow, and Peking) give Moscow any lasting protection from Peking?

No one knows better than does the Kremlin that the signature of Peking (or any other Communist government) on such a document would be worthless. After all, it was the Kremlin which *taught* the Peking regime that only fools honor any agreement when it fails to give them an advantage.

Incidentally, no matter how sincerely the Kremlin might *want* to honor the Nixon-Brezhnev Arms Limitation Agreement, it simply can't *afford* to do so for the full five years if Peking should prove able to sharply step up *its* nuclear weapons program.

D. What about Moscow's imagined option of merely "kissing Peking along" until a propaganda-weakened U.S. could be bluffed into submission?

The first thing wrong with such an alleged option is that Peking just isn't stupid enough to wait that long. Peking undoubtedly has its "period of most favorable odds" closely calculated by now and knows that if it is to escape complete humiliation by and total subservience to Moscow it must make its final play long *before* the U.S. could possibly be bluffed into submission and used to bolster the Kremlin's position.

The second thing wrong with such a Moscow option is that, although U.S. self-confidence has been badly undermined by indirect Soviet manipulation of many U.S. newsmen and officials, the American people will fight to the death when they fully realize what is being done to them.

The third reason why such a gambit cannot save the Russians from a final nuclear showdown with the Chinese is that any "final ultimatum" by the Kremlin to the U.S. *before* Peking's nuclear arsenal is "adequate," would leave the Soviet Union so terribly depleted as to make it "easy pickings" for even *today's* level of Chinese armament.

And, of course, even if Moscow *could* actually bluff the U.S. into early submission (and then use its augmented advantage to bluff Peking into submission), Moscow's resulting "world government" would, as previously demonstrated, always be at the mercy of *individual* smugglers who could blackmail it into impotence.

In short, just coasting along on its *present* course cannot protect Moscow from a final nuclear showdown with Peking.

E. The only option (for coping with the Chinese threat) that can give Moscow an acceptable alternative *to attempted world conquest—the only option,* other *than world conquest, that can come anywhere near guaranteeing the Soviet Union complete security from all foreign interference in its internal affairs, is a Unaforce.*

It has long been a basic tenet of the various "Communist" creeds that, in order to maintain its power over its *own* people, any Communist government must carefully shield them from exposure to any viewpoints other than its own. And, up to now, there has been no sure way to accomplish that *except* by getting all the world under one government which it can control. But the kind of Unaforce here proposed would not only protect the Soviet (and Peking) governments from all foreign interference in their domestic affairs, it would also give to Moscow and Peking, as well as all other governments so inclined, the privilege of "shutting out" foreign ideas as much as it pleased. Under a Unaforce as here proposed, every nation would be privileged to punish as it saw fit any foreign secret agent within its boundaries, without fear of reprisal by anyone. Of course any nation which earned a reputation for mistaking ordinary tourists and commercial travelers for foreign agents would thereby sharply lessen its income from tourists and foreign trade. But it would be fully protected in that privilege.

Also, under a Unaforce every nation that chose to do so would be privileged to operate "jamming equipment" designed to prevent its own people from receiving foreign broadcasts. Of course if jamming equipment were used by (for instance) Moscow in such a way as to seriously affect broadcast reception in *neighboring* countries, those countries would no doubt retaliate in kind. But, in no case would Unaforce be permitted to tolerate any *military* threats by either side.

With such provisions in the Unaforce charter, no one could seriously interfere with any government's "thought control" over its *own* people. Those few nations now attempting to exercise a high degree of such control would gradually develop to a point where either control was no longer needed or their own people would no longer tolerate it.

Of these five Soviet options for attempting to avoid nuclear disaster, only the last one, that of a Unaforce, would seem to offer Moscow (and Peking and the U.S.) any real hope of escaping endless exposure to nuclear blackmail and/or nuclear wipeout. More detailed support for that assertion will be forthcoming. But let's pause here for another of our 14 truths.

VIII. NO NATION CAN *NOW* HOPE TO GAIN AS MUCH *ADVANTAGE* FROM ATTEMPTED WORLD CONQUEST AS IT COULD FROM A *DEPENDABLE* GUARANTEE OF SECURITY FROM FOREIGN INTERFERENCE IN ITS DOMESTIC AFFAIRS AND FROM MASS ANNIHILATION.

If we can convincingly demonstrate the truth of that statement, then there should be a real possibility of getting the support of at least the Washington and Moscow axes for a fully bluff-proof and acceptably subversion-proof Unaforce. But to develop at all convincingly the truth of any statement involving such vast ramifications requires the correlation of many *other* little-recognized truths, some of which we have not yet had time and space even to identify. Just hold this truth VIII in the back of your mind until we can review all the rest of the material needed to support it. But with this truth VIII in mind, it should surprise no one that such spokesmen for the U.S. radical left as Arthur Waskow of the Institute for Policy Studies have recently been *urging* the creation of an impregnably-armed international police agency. By offering (as a *political* control mechanism for such an agency) only some modification of the present U.N., such left-wingers naturally arouse suspicion of their *motives* by the U.S. "silent majority." Certainly the U.S. delegates to any conference for negotiating a Unaforce charter would have to be screened with *exceeding* care. But a U.S. delegation truly dedicated to the continued *independence* of today's "free" nations would hold out "to the bitter end" for the special kind of charter herein sketched, which could make a Unaforce *less* of a risk for every nation than every nation must now face *without* a bluff-proof international agency to protect it.

IX. RED CHINA'S APPROVAL OF THE KIND OF UNAFORCE CHARTER HEREIN PROPOSED WOULD NOT BE ESSENTIAL TO ITS ADOPTION AND FAITHFUL OPERATION. THE "WORLD VOTING PATTERN" PROPOSED FURTHER ON IN THESE PAGES WOULD ENABLE THE U.S., THE U.S.S.R., AND THEIR PRINCIPAL ALLIES TO PUT SUCH A PROGRAM IN OPERATION IN THE NEXT COUPLE OF YEARS, WITH OR *WITHOUT* PEKING'S CONSENT. NEVERTHELESS, SUCH A PROGRAM WOULD INSURE TO THE CHINESE ALL THE SAME BENEFITS AS TO THE WORLD'S OTHER NATIONS.

Actually, nothing the Peking regime could ever hope to accomplish by its *own* use of nuclear weapons could give it as "glorious" a place in history as it could earn by devoting all its energies (and most of its military budget) to helping its own people realize their very great potential under Unaforce protection.

X. IF (EVEN WITHOUT A NUCLEAR EXCHANGE) THE NEVER-ABSENT *THREAT* OF SUDDEN BODILY

HARM CAN TURN MOST HUMANS INTO USE-
LESS EMOTIONAL CRIPPLES—AND IF THAT
THREAT CAN NEVER BE ENDED BY ANY NA-
TIONAL OR WORLD "GOVERNMENT" WITH
NON-MILITARY TARGETS OF ITS OWN—THEN
THE WORLD CANNOT CONTINUE TO "MUDDLE
THROUGH" WITHOUT A FULLY BLUFF-PROOF
"UNAFORCE."

The nations always *have* been able to "muddle through"
without any bluff-proof central authority to keep them off each
other's backs. They never *have* had to commit themselves in
advance to any rigid pattern of central controls. Why can't they
just go on muddling through. Now that nuclear weapons will
soon be in the hands of people far less cautious and with far
"less to lose" than those of the U.S. and U.S.S.R., a world without rigid *central* control over the new mass weapons will be in
much the position of a moon-rocket crew without any "ground
central." Unlike the world leaders of the past, today's pilots of
nuclear-armed nations and of moon-rockets will have no second
chance to profit by early mistakes. There is simply no time left
to plan for survival *after* the launching of moon-rockets or
nuclear weapons. This new breed of pilots must allow themselves
to be bound in *advance* by some rigid central discipline—or
perish. Each nation *can* still "muddle through" as regards its
domestic affairs, but the split-second decisions regarding the use
of nuclear weapons must now be made in *advance* by the wording of a world charter, if anyone's life is to be worth living.
    Can any world-security mechanism accomplish its objective
without the fully plausible threat of *force*? Not until nearly all
adult human bodies are inhabited by emotionally mature minds.
When will that be? Expecting all nuclear-armed nations to "be-
have themselves" without a fully plausible threat of force is as
silly as expecting that the "school bully" at your old grade school
could be "sweet-talked" into behaving himself if he found there
was no inescapable penalty for pushing his schoolmates around.
    The key political problems of the nuclear age then, are:

(a) how to insure that the penalty for international aggression is an absolutely inescapable penalty, and (b) *how to insure that the disciplinary mechanism cannot be "taken over" by those it was designed to discipline.*

Certain little-recognized truths now make it possible to safeguard a Unaforce from misuse at least as well as the U.S. military establishment was safeguarded when *that* body had a world monopoly of the new mass weapons. Unfortunately, these truths are not self-evident and are interdependent for part of their validity. So they may sound implausible until *all* of them have been studied and correlated. The first of these special truths pertaining to a Unaforce charter is that:

XI. ITS CHARTER CAN BE SO WORDED THAT A UNAFORCE COULD NOT GREATLY *WRONG* ANY NATION EXCEPT BY ACTUALLY *VIOLATING ITS OWN CHARTER.*

SINCE ANY MAJOR CHARTER VIOLATION WOULD INSTANTLY DEPRIVE EVERY NATION OF THE ONLY REAL SECURITY FROM FOREIGN DOMINATION THAT IT HAD EVER HAD (OR COULD EVER HOPE TO HAVE), THE ONLY NATIONS THAT WOULD EVER *WANT* UNAFORCE TO VIOLATE ITS CHARTER WOULD BE ONES BENT ON WORLD CONQUEST.

If the above statements are true, then it is evident that the most basic remaining problem (in safeguarding a Unaforce against takeover) is how to insure that at least two thirds of all Unaforce officers and men would always truly represent nations *opposed* to any given scheme of world conquest. This can be done. But before trying to show how, let's examine some of the reasons behind the *first statement* (that a Unaforce could not greatly wrong any nation except by actually violating its charter).

Because the kind of Unaforce here proposed would have no major responsibility or authority except to impose certain very precisely defined penalties prescribed by the charter for certain precisely defined acts of international aggression listed in the charter, a Unaforce would not need to be given any very major decision-making powers. The infinitely complex problems of family life, of economics, of equitable taxation, of unemployment, and the like, which necessitate most of the decisions made by any "government" or city police force, would not be within the province of a Unaforce. All of those Unaforce actions, the consequences of which might be of major significance to the world, could be decided *for* it in advance by the wording of its charter and/or by a separate "World Emergency Court." Such a court would of course need (at least as badly as would Unaforce itself) adequate safeguards from subversion and takeover. Such safeguards (having much the same roots as those herein proposed for the reliable control of Unaforce personnel) are closely examined further on.

But Unaforce could thus be relieved of major decision-making power *only* if the Unaforce charter also embodied a set of enforceable *boundary lines* for each of the nations. Back in 1945 when the U.N. charter was being planned, many nations would *not* have agreed to the freezing of the status quo as regarded their national boundary lines. At that time (with "safe old Uncle Sam" holding a nuclear monopoly), they felt they could afford to wrangle endlessly over ancient territorial claims. But those comfortable days are now long gone. And if it is true that only a fully-proof international agency can end the daily threat of mass annihilation (and if such an agency cannot be acceptably safeguarded from takeover *without* including enforceable and "permanent" boundary lines into its charter), then the necessary proportion of the nations *can* be shown the wisdom of settling for status quo boundary lines in the charter. To repeat, now that a given nation can be shown it has no chance to escape the daily threat of surprise annihilation *except* by supporting some sort of Unaforce, and when it can be shown that such an international enforcement agency can be adequately safeguarded from takeover *only* by including each nation's enforceable boundary lines in its charter, then the idea of status quo boundary lines becomes a "salable" one.

Another reason a Unaforce could be almost completely relieved of responsibility and of authority for major decisions is that, unlike any other "army," Unaforce would never be "at war." Its absolutely invincible military position would be so obvious to even the dizziest little dictator that the Unaforce command would never *need* to make the on-the-spot field strategy decisions necessary for ordinary military men. If some nation were actually reckless enough to try to test the resolve of the Unaforce Command (and if the Unaforce satellite and other surveillance equipment failed to show "beyond possible doubt" that such nation was a "punishable aggressor" as defined by the charter), then Unaforce would have no power to impose the charter-prescribed penalties until the World Emergency Court had weighed the evidence and *ordered* Unaforce to carry out its charter-prescribed penalties.

These are some of the reasons that the kind of Unaforce more fully "blueprinted" in later pages could not greatly wrong any nation except by actually *violating its own charter*.

The charter would of course provide that, although no nation's charter boundaries could be changed by threat of force, all nations would under prescribed conditions have the privilege of *voluntary* merger or split-up. Whether or not such action was indeed voluntary would be decided not by Unaforce, but by the World Emergency Court. The charter would also provide that any nation voluntarily adopting a Communist government would thereby automatically transfer itself to the Communist Voting Bloc. But what if (by such automatic transfers) Communist "Bloc A" eventually included the *majority* of all the world's nations? Most unlikely. Under Unaforce every nation would not only be protected from open threats but would be privileged to deal with terrorist infiltrators in any way it saw fit, *without* fear of reprisal. Almost none of the nations now fully *exposed* to such foreign pressures have given in and adopted Communist governments, and they would be far *less* likely to do so when fully protected from all foreign pressures.

If a majority of the nations ever *did* voluntarily transfer themselves to the Communist Voting Bloc, it would be only because "Communism" had *matured* to a point where it was an

acceptable way of life to a "free" people. To provide for that
remote eventuality, the original charter could provide for "automatic" adjustment of its amendment procedure if and when
either of the "great power" Voting Blocs contained a majority
of all the world's nations. Space here does not permit detailing
all such refinements of a Unaforce charter, but they *can* be
worked out so as to make a Unaforce charter far less risky for
every nation than are *any* of the world's present alternatives.

XII. IF ALL THE NATIONS OF THE WORLD WERE
GROUPED INTO JUST THREE VOTING BLOCS
AND EACH BLOC HAD ONLY ONE SINGLE VOTE
(THE NATURE OF WHICH WOULD BE DECIDED
BY A PLURALITY OF THE HEADS OF STATE IN
THAT BLOC), THEN THOSE NATIONS TO WHICH
THE "BALANCE OF POWER" VOTE COULD MOST
SAFELY BE GIVEN WOULD BE THE 80 OR SO LEAST
DEVELOPED, LEAST PROSPEROUS, AND MOST
DEFENSELESS NATIONS.

If Voting Bloc A consisted of all the nations with Communist governments and Bloc B consisted of all the more industrialized, prosperous nations of the "free world," these two
Blocs would desperately need protection from each *other,* as at
present. Remembering, then, that any nation's or individual's
attempted conquest of other nations would necessitate *violation*
of the kind of Unaforce charter here proposed, it becomes apparent that the only kind of Voting Bloc C that could protect
Blocs A and B from each other, would be one composed of
nations that would always *lose far more than they could hope to
gain by a charter violation* that again exposed them to would-be
conquerors.

It is inconceivable that anywhere near a plurality of these
80 or so "weakest" nations would ever swing their one Bloc Vote
behind anything or anybody suspected of favoring attempted
conquest. The evidence is conclusive that practically all such
nations value their "right of self-determination" far more than

they do any of the "riches-power-and-glory" bait now being dangled before them by such would-be world-conquerors as Moscow and Peking. Almost none of them have yielded to the terrific current pressures to adopt Communist governments and thereby put themselves under foreign domination. Under a Unaforce no one could apply to the 80 or so "underprivileged" nations in Voting Bloc C the kind of pressures to which they are *now* exposed. So they would be even *less* likely than at present to support any action that might again expose them to the whims of "empire builders."

If, then, Bloc C were made up of those many nations that best know how it actually feels to be under the heel of a conqueror (and that are now proving beyond doubt that nothing short of brute force can get them to accept foreign domination), our three Voting Blocs would provide the right "cornerstone" for a safe and effective world peace force. "But," you say, "if nearly all of the nations to be included in Voting Bloc C actually do value their right to govern themselves, more than they value any possible bribe from a world-conqueror, why are so many of the Arab nations, for instance, allowing themselves to be bribed by the Kremlin?" Bribed to do what? If they were doing what Moscow is *trying* to bribe them to do, they would all have adopted Communist governments long ago, thereby putting themselves under Moscow's domination. But they steadfastly refuse to do what Moscow most wants. Instead, Moscow is doing what the Arabs want—helping them fight the Israelis. Of course the Arabs are taking serious risks when they accept such massive aid from the Russians. But they will not have been successfully bribed unless they eventually break down and relinquish their right to control of their own government. If that ever happens, it obviously won't be due to the riches Moscow is pouring on them but only because there will be no one to *protect* them from eventual threats of brute force by their present "benefactor."

Under a Unaforce charter they *would* have complete protection from such a "benefactor's" threats of force. And since, under the type of charter here proposed, the terms "charter violation" and "attempted world conquest" would be practically synonymous, it would be a very safe bet that such a Bloc C would never support any other Bloc bent on violating the charter, thereby exposing these underprivileged nations to foreign threats of force. Any charter violation would leave the 80 or so "weak" nations in Bloc C once more at the mercy of the merciless; and, because they would be keenly aware of that fact, they could be trusted not to nominate anyone to the Unaforce staff or to the Emergency Court whom *they* did not feel they could depend on to oppose any conquest conspiracy, i.e., charter violation.

But how can we make sure that some of the Unaforce staff nominated by the two Blocs certain to be opposed to any given charter violation would not later *betray* the interests of the Bloc which nominated them? No matter how rigidly the charter required such men to be screened (to eliminate the stupid, the weak, the uneducated, the emotionally unstable), no matter how much better they were *paid* than any present military or police force, no matter how fully they were protected by charter provisions from "hurt pride," no matter how much honor, prestige, and *esprit de corps* any traitor to Unaforce would be sacrificing —a very few might eventually be bribed or blackmailed into acting against the interests of the Voting Bloc that had nominated them. But the total number of such potential turncoats would be trival as compared to the number in any present army. Even if 5% or 10% of all the Unaforce men nominated by the two Blocs opposed to a given charter violation proved vulnerable to blackmail or bribery, we can be sure that these would be at least *balanced* by Unaforce men from the "conspirator's" Bloc, whose personal integrity and pride in their Unaforce careers would *outweigh* their loyalty to a homeland engaged in trying to destroy world peace, especially because all competent and faithful Unaforce personnel would be secure for *life* with Unaforce, not only financially secure but possessed of a degree of status, honor, and prestige that they would be very slow to risk.

If we are safe in assuming that a plurality of the *nations* in each of two of the Voting Blocs would always be in opposition to any nation's attempted "world-grab," then we can also safely assume that two thirds of the *Unaforce* staff would also be in opposition to such a "grab." And the faithful two thirds of the Unaforce staff would be under inescapable charter-obligation to arrest and remove from Unaforce premises for future trial (or if necessary, shoot) any of their comrades suspected of conspiracy to violate the charter. Such suspects would be convicted or reinstated by the World Emergency Court. Since each Voting Bloc would control the appointment of five of the Court's fifteen members, the balance of power in this Court would parallel that among the Blocs themselves. Hence two thirds of the Court Justices would be appointees of (and subject to instant impeachment by) the two Voting Blocs certain to be in opposition to any given attempt to violate the charter. Remember that the kind of charter here proposed would make charter violation practically *synonymous* with attempted world conquest.

But what if Court Justices or their families or Unaforce officers or their families were kidnapped or threatened with bodily harm in order to influence the decisions of such officials? The reason that political assassination and kipnapping are *now* a serious threat to all organized society is that the *penalty* for this intolerable crime is neither realistic nor inescapable. We have seen in recent years that at least some of the world's secret services can almost infallibly identify and capture any criminal worth their all-out effort. The breakdown of justice for political kidnappers and assassins is due to the fact that court procedures and penalties suitable for local crime in a simpler age are wholly inadequate to cope with international *conspiracies*. If, for instance, the Uruguayan government (instead of releasing the twenty or so prisoners whose release was demanded by the kidnappers of the Swiss ambassador) had announced that the prisoners whose release was sought would all be executed within three days if the Ambassador was not released, he would have been released. Such action by the government would *not* have been unjust because by demanding the release of those specific prisoners the kidnappers officially identified them as members of their criminal conspiracy.

Governments whose legal systems are not geared to the realities of today's world *invite* crime by their vacillation. But a Unaforce *could* not vacillate. Its charter would make clear that any attempt to pressure Emergency Court Justices or Unaforce officers into betraying their trust would rate as the greatest of crimes against all the world's people and that anyone and everyone actively participating in a conspiracy to commit such crime would die for it. Once the Emergency Court had weighed the evidence and found an individual guilty of participation in a plot to threaten Unaforce or Court officials, it would have no responsibility for choosing the penalty. The charter itself would require Unaforce to execute all such criminals and imprison their nearest of kin. If the evidence clearly showed that some *national government* was behind the plot, Unaforce would have no option but to destroy specified important targets in that nation. When the punishment really fits the crime and is known in advance to be an *inescapable* penalty, that crime just is not committed, except possibly by an isolated madman who is no very serious threat to society as a whole. Many of the devices that would be needed to fully safeguard an Emergency Court, the Bloc Administrative Commissions, and Unaforce officers from corruption cannot be properly spelled out in an article of this length, but such devices are available and adequate.

What about the matter of "economic aggression"? Could the Bloc C nations for instance, protect themselves from *that* kind of aggression? Certainly. The Unaforce charter would not permit any nation to be physically punished for expropriating foreign investments within its borders. Of course any nation foolish enough to *grossly* mistreat its foreign investors would thereby probably end its chances of getting needed help in the future. But no "have" nation could, under the Unaforce charter, control the internal resources of any "have-not" nation, except to the extent that the latter deemed to be in its own best long-range interests.

Certainly there has never been and can never be any pattern of human organization that can be made *absolutely* "fail-safe." In selecting such a pattern we can only choose between what appear to be the greater and lesser *risks*. The writer believes that the safeguards available for a Unaforce and a World Emergency

Court can reduce the risk of establishing those entities to a fraction of the risks every nation is *now* facing.

XIII. THE ONE MOST *IMPORTANT* TOOL USED BY POWER-GRABBERS OF THE PAST (TO SUBVERT AND TAKE OVER EXISTING GOVERNMENTS) WOULD NOT BE *AVAILABLE* TO ANY WOULD-BE SUBVERTER OF THE KIND OF UNAFORCE HERE PROPOSED.

Napoleon could not have taken control of the French government, Lenin and Trotsky could not have taken over Russia, and Hitler could not have taken over Germany had they not been able to use the one chief tool of all subverters. Without it, they would have been laughed into obscurity by the level-headed majority in those nations. But each of those revolutionaries could *plausibly blame* the existing government for failure—failure to ameliorate poverty and injustice, failure to reduce taxes, failure to improve housing and roads, failure to win a past war, failure to prepare for a next war, failure to improve the prison system, and so on. By contrast, the kind of Unaforce here proposed could never be plausibly accused of such failures. Everyone would know that Unaforce had no responsibility whatever for the domestic woes of any nation. Its *only* responsibility or authority would be to impose charter-prescribed penalties for charter-defined acts of international aggression. Hence it could not plausibly be accused of any great failure or wrongdoing except the *violation of its own charter*. How far could a power-mad conspirator get by *blaming* Unaforce for failure to violate its own charter? How many Unaforce men could he win over to his cause by *any* means other than bribery or blackmail, unless they were from the same homeland or Voting Bloc as he was? How could he hope to win over *all* of even those Unaforce men from his own homeland when he could not plausibly blame Unaforce for any failures? He would have to rely on bribery and blackmail to build any very dangerous following, and both these devices can be far better guarded against by a Unaforce charter than by any "government's" constitution. Only men of very dubious character can be bribed or blackmailed into betraying their oath of office to the great detriment of their homelands. Well, doesn't every "army" *have* a lot of men of dubious character? Undoubtedly. But no national army or police force can *afford* to pay all its men like corporation executives. Because Unaforce would need only a tiny fraction of the total manpower in all of today's national armies, its comparatively small staff of technical experts and officers could (and must) be paid so very well and given such extraordinary "fringe benefits" that bribes of mere money could hardly induce them to risk their lives and incur the world's hatred by helping a power-grabber who would probably turn out to be a loser anyway.

How about Unaforce men who (in spite of history's most rigid screening process) might *later* develop the neurotic power-madness of a Hitler or a Stalin? The youthful bitterness and frustration that drove such men to commit such crimes against their fellow men were already fully apparent *before* they ever reached positions of power. Any good psychologist who had minutely examined their youthful records would have recognized that they were probably headed for big trouble. The Unaforce charter would spell out a screening process that would prevent nearly all such frustrated and potentially power-mad individuals from ever getting *onto* the Unaforce staff. It would also provide that every Unaforce candidate have a specified high level of I.Q., a broad and thorough education, and a record of fully reliable performance in one of the needed technical or professional fields. In short, the proportion of the total Unaforce staff that could be bribed with dubious promises of even *more* power and glory to betray their trust would be trivial as compared to the size of the total staff. When at least two thirds of an army's top command and two thirds of its lower echelons as well are faithful to their duty and when part of their charter duty is to arrest (or if necessary kill) any of their fellows suspected of treasonable conspiracy, that army is on pretty safe ground.

A Hitler or an Eldridge Cleaver *becomes* a revolutionary primarily because of "hurt pride." If a Unaforce officer were repeatedly passed over for promotion, might not his hurt pride prompt him to listen to some conspirator? Possibly. For this reason, the charter should provide that any Unaforce officer who (above a certain level) had to be "passed over" more than twice would be automatically retired on two-thirds pay regardless of his age, unless he deserved a dishonorable discharge. The world could well afford the luxury of such an arrangement to protect itself.

As to the possibility of blackmailing Unaforce men for their past indiscretions, that would be easy to prevent. Whereas any poorly-paid and carelessly recruited national army (or government) has *many* men in fairly high places who are vulnerable to blackmail, the one out of thousands of candidates who actually got into the Unaforce staff would have had every day and act of his life so thoroughly investigated (by *each* Bloc's "Bloc Administrative Commission") that few indeed of such men could have anything left to hide and to be blackmailed for.

XIV. A UNAFORCE WOULD HAVE A VERY HIGH DEGREE OF *"AUTOMATIC"* SECURITY FROM TAKEOVER, A KIND OF SECURITY NO "GOVERNMENT" EVER HAS HAD OR EVER COULD HAVE.

The big reason why a Unaforce is needed in the first place is that only such a "possessionless" agency can be made *bluffproof*. But if the Unaforce Governor-General, for instance, should suddenly lose his sanity and try to set himself up as a world dictator, he would thereby take direct control of the world's nonmilitary assets, which would cost "his" Unaforce its former invulnerability to successful blackmail. His homeland or any other of "his" new assets could then be held hostage by a few private individuals capable of smuggling mass-weapons components. In such event, such components would be *especially* easy to come by, because the charter would require Unaforce to prorate its contract purchases of mass weapons among at least two of the three Voting Blocs. So long as Unaforce *remained* "possessionless" and bluff-proof, these Unaforce suppliers could be no men-

ace. But the minute Unaforce lost its invulnerability (by taking
control of any non-military assets), such weapons in the hands
of the contract suppliers would enable private individuals to
play havoc with Unaforce's illegal new boss.

Even if a Unaforce Governor-General "gone mad" should
attempt such a coup, he would have no luck getting the support
of the rest of his top command against such fantastic odds. He
would be shot down by his saner associates before he could do
any very serious harm. They would recognize that what he was
attempting to do would put the world right back where it was
before Unaforce was created—nowhere.

XV. ACTUAL *FIRING* OF UNAFORCE WEAPONS WOULD PROBABLY NEVER BE NECESSARY.

Humanity would gain little by a Unaforce if (in order to
enforce the charter's anti-aggression laws) Unaforce had to *fire*
a lot of its nuclear weapons every few years. But there is almost
no chance that the kind of Unaforce here proposed would ever
have to use any but its "conventional" weapons. The main
reason nuclear weapons are now such a ghastly menace to
humanity is that under present conditions, a reckless nation might
hope to inflict a lot more damage than it would sustain in a
nuclear exchange. As long as there is even one chance in a
hundred that an aggressor would "win" by a nuclear exchange,
there will be some fool ready to takes that chance. But with the
kind of Unaforce here proposed, everyone would know in
advance *beyond all possible doubt* that no one could ever win a
nuclear battle with Unaforce. Therefore it would never be
attempted.

What *would* probably happen during the early years of a
Unaforce is that some nuclear power would indulge in a sly
attempt to test the firmness of Unaforce resolve by committing
one of the minor acts of aggression for which the charter provided a relatively mild punishment. The evidence would not be
sufficiently clear-cut to permit *any* action by Unaforce until such
evidence had been weighed by the World Emergency Court. But

the charter would not give the Court any leeway to judge of the "wisdom" of the charter. That would already have been determined by concordance among all three Blocs before the charter was signed. The Court could only pass on the validity or invalidity of the evidence that action of the accused did or did not constitute a violation of one of the charter-defined "acts of punishable aggression." Then, if the Court found the accused nation guilty, Unaforce would be inescapably bound to impose the prescribed penalty for that offense. Perhaps that particular penalty would involve ordering the offending nation to clear all personnel out of its three largest industrial complexes preparatory to their destruction by Unaforce fire and TNT bombs. Only if the aggressor then counter-attacked Unaforce, would Unaforce be privileged and required to use its nuclear weapons. And no such massive counterattack would ever occur when the aggressor knew in advance, beyond all possible doubt, that it had *no* chance of winning. With such a Unaforce charter in effect, it is hardly conceivable that Unaforce would *ever* have occasion to fire any of its *nuclear* weapons.

HUMANITY'S ONE MOST *PRESSING* TASK

Eliminating poverty, cutting the birth rate, saving the ecology, improving race relations—all these are very pressing jobs we must undertake. But unless nuclear blackmail can very soon be brought under rigid control, all else will be of slight consequence. Now that you have briefly examined the *relationships* between the various "truths" here presented, you need to make up your mind, before going any further, if the *first* seven of these truths are indeed substantially true. If they are, then nothing *but* a fully bluff-proof international agency (having no non-military assets to be held hostage) can ever hope to end the daily threat to human survival. And if this last statement is true, then humanity's one most *pressing* task is the completion of a type of charter that can make the nuclear arming of a "Unaforce" the *lesser* risk.

Unaforce Organization Chart

Because Unaforce itself would have no substantial deliberative or judicial functions—no responsibility for complex decisions regarding care of the poor, crime in the streets, taxation, education, and the like—its authority to punish international aggression could be so precisely defined by its charter that it could not very seriously harm any nation except by *violating its charter*. The next problem then, is how to make as certain as possible that at least a plurality of the Unaforce officers and manpower would never *want* to see the charter violated. To accomplish this, we have grouped all nations into three very special kinds of "Voting Blocs," as shown by the Organization Chart—each Bloc with only one vote, the nature of which would be determined by a plurality of the "Heads of State" of the nations in that Bloc. Adoption (and later amendment) of the charter itself would require all three of these Bloc Votes. But only two of the three Bloc votes would be required to elect each member of the Unaforce "High Command." Each Bloc would independently elect its own Bloc Administrative Commission and its own share of Justices on the World Emergency Court. Each Bloc's one third of the total Unaforce manpower would be rigidly screened to exacting charter specifications and "nominated" by that Bloc's Administrative Commission and would be subject to final appointment or rejection by the Unaforce High Command.

Now, considering the makeup of each of the three Voting Blocs shown in the chart, is it conceivable that *more* than one of these Voting Blocs would ever (by a two-thirds vote of all its nations) favor any aggressor's scheme to steal full control of Unaforce and make it violate its charter? Doing so would wreck the only real security from foreign aggression such nations had

ever had or could ever hope to have. And so long as two of these
Blocs (represented by two-thirds of the total Unaforce manpower) were *against* such subversion and charter violation, every
would-be defector on the Unaforce staff would have at his elbow
at least *two* associates under oath to arrest (or, if necessary, to
shoot) him.

Remember that, because Unaforce could never be blamed for
any of the complex domestic troubles of any nation, a would-be
subverter of Unaforce would have none of the kinds of "ammunition of unrest" with which a Hitler was able to mislead the
ignorant and unstable. Remember also, that no really stupid,
uneducated, or emotionally unstable individuals could clear all
the hurdles to get *on* the Unaforce staff. This voting-control
pattern and type of charter could actually make a militarily invulnerable Unaforce far safer for every nation than is the situation it
now faces without a Unaforce.

As the passing years changed the literacy, economic, and
political status of nations, each would be privileged to seek transfer
to one of the other two Blocs, but only in relation to rules
detailed in the charter. These rules could substantially insure
that, at *all* times, the nations in Bloc C would be those with the
least to gain and the most to lose by any violation of the charter.

The nominees for the three top Unaforce spots would (after
the initial ten years of operation) all be seasoned Unaforce
veterans, the world's highest paid and most soundly motivated
soldiers. As compared to any military force of the past, the
Unaforce staff would have infinitely more reason for pride in, and
respect for, their organization. Such unparalleled *esprit de corps*
would represent a very tough nut for any would-be subverter to
crack. But any Unaforce man suspected of attempting or con-
spring to violate the charter would be subject to instant "preliminary impeachment" and prompt removal from Unaforce
premises, subject to formal trial by the World Emergency Court.
And such defensive actions could be initiated not only by any
member of the Unaforce staff but also by a two-thirds vote of
the three Bloc Administrative Commissions.

The decisions or conduct of any World Emergency Court

VOTING CONTROL PATTERN AND "SYSTEM OF CHECKS AND BALANCES"
FOR "WORLD ANTI-AGGRESSION ENFORCEMENT AGENCY" ("UNAFORCE")

VOTING BLOC A

All Communist-affiliated nations, present and future:

Soviet Union, China, East Germany, North Korea, Poland, Yugoslavia, and so on.

A plurality of all Chiefs of State in the Bloc would determine the nature of the three top Unaforce officers, for each of five of the Court members, and for each member of their own Administrative Commission.

VOTING BLOC B

All those industrialized "Free-World" nations having high levels of literacy, where the votes of the masses can greatly influence government policy:

United States, Canada, most of Western Europe, Australia, Japan, Israel, and so on.

Voting procedure same as for Bloc A.

VOTING BLOC C

All remaining nations—the "under-developed" ones and the *non*-Communist dictatorships:

India, Spain, Iran, Panama, the Sudan, South Vietnam, Brazil, and so on.

Voting procedure same as for Bloc A.

BLOC A'S NINE-MAN "BLOC ADMINISTRATIVE COMMISSION"

Functions same as for Bloc B commission.

Although these three "Commissions" would (by a two-thirds vote) *nominate* the three candidates for the Unaforce "High Command," the final election of these offices would be by the "Heads of State" in the three Voting Blocs—each Bloc having but one single vote, the nature of which would be determined by two-thirds of the Heads of State in that Bloc.

BLOC B'S NINE-MAN "BLOC ADMINISTRATIVE COMMISSION"

Would screen and nominate this Bloc's one-third of total candidates for Unaforce staff, subject to appointment or rejection by the Unaforce High Command.

This group plus either of the other two Bloc Commissions could order arrest of any Unaforce officer suspected of attempting or conspiring to violate the Unaforce charter and hold him for trial by the World Emergency Court. Because of its limited scope of responsibilities, its decisions could require plurality.

Any two of these Bloc Commissions could block any given purchase-contract by Unaforce beyond some specified amount. Safeguards against subversion of this body to be found in Answers to Question 10, pages 109-12.

BLOC C'S NINE-MAN "BLOC ADMINISTRATIVE COMMISSION"

Functions same as for Bloc B commission.

See pages 56-57, 60 for short summary of principles involved.

15-MEMBER "WORLD EMERGENCY COURT"

Incontrovertible evidence that one nation had threatened another with physical force or attacked it—or that a fully identified nation had attacked Unaforce—or that a Unaforce man had attempted or conspired to violate the charter—would enable Unaforce to issue prescribed warnings and/or impose charter-prescribed penalties *without* reference to this court. But where evidence of such offense warranted a court hearing, Unaforce action would be decided by this court, by a plurality vote.

Five of the court's fifteen members would be elected by each Voting Bloc. Each member would be subject to quick preliminary impeachment by any two of the three Bloc Administrative Commissions. Final impeachment or reinstatement would be by a plurality of the Heads of State in each of *two* of the Voting Blocs.

GOVERNOR-GENERAL OF UNAFORCE

Responsible (with staff below) for issuing prescribed warning to, and/or imposing prescribed penalty on any nation that threatened use of force against another nation or committed an act defined by the charter as "aggression."

To insure that Blocs B and C between them could not deny to Bloc A fair representation on the Unaforce High Command, the charter would provide that the three members of the High Command must always be from three *different* Blocs.

UNAFORCE STAFF

One-third nominated by, and representative of, each of the three Voting Blocs through their Administrative Commissions, subject to appointment or rejection by High Command. Staff members subject to arrest and instant removal for conspiring to violate charter.

CHIEF OF STAFF

LIEUTENANT-GOVERNOR

Justice would be subject to "instant challenge" by any two of the Bloc Administrative Commissions, and the final decision to replace or exonerate such a justice would be made by two thirds of the "Heads of State" in each of *two* of the Voting Blocs.

When the proposed system of voting control was reinforced by such a system of checks and balances, the risk to each nation of this Unaforce program could be far less than the risk each now faces without a Unaforce. When it was known beyond doubt by all nations that Unaforce not only could but also *must,* infallibly impose insupportable penalties for violation of its charter laws, Unaforce would never *have* to actually use its nuclear weapons.

Question and Answer Appendix

Much of what is needed to make a Unaforce "the lesser risk" (detailed charter provisions and many of the arguments needed to fully support statements already made) will be found in the appendix that follows. Previous pages omitted some of these essential, but perhaps tiresome, "trees" to give the reader a quicker, clearer view of the "forest." Not even the appendix that follows (nor any one whole book of "readable" length) can hope to deal adequately with every one of the possible "ifs and buts" regarding *safe* operation of a Unaforce. But the reasoning here presented and the safeguarding techniques here proposed should be sufficient to get the world's ablest statesmen and military technicians excited about completing the job—without fatal delay.

Before getting lost in the detail of any one answer, please read thoughtfully the *whole list of questions,* as follows:

1. Why can't the U.N. ever be trusted with nuclear weapons? *See answer on pages 63-64.*
2. Why and how can a "Unaforce" be made fully bluff-proof (and therefore *capable* of enforcing anti-aggression laws) when given the same weapons that could *not* make the U.N. or any national or world "government" bluff-proof? *See answer on pages 64-69.*
3. Why could not the kind of Unaforce here proposed seriously wrong any nation without actually *violating its charter? See answer on pages 69-70.*
4. How can a militarily invulnerable Unaforce be prevented from violating its charter and becoming the private tool of some aggression-minded nation? *See answers on pages 70-85.*
5. How can some power-mad officer of Unaforce itself be prevented from using the Unaforce power to make himself a world dictator? *See answers on pages 85-88.*

6. Why can't the "Great Powers" (Voting Blocs A and B as herein constituted) hope to protect themselves from each other except by giving the world's *third* vote (the Bloc C vote) to the "underdeveloped" nations? And how can these 80 or so "hungry" nations in Block C be prevented from using their "balance of power" vote to "rob" the more prosperous nations in the other two Blocs?
   See answers on pages 88-96.

7. Precisely how can "punishable aggression" be clearly and safely defined by a Unaforce charter? And why could the short-sighted hairsplitting that kept adequate anti-aggression laws out of the U.N. charter now be overcome?
   See answers on pages 96-105.

8. If Unaforce were notified that one nation was subtly threatening another with military action, who would decide if the evidence supplied by the accuser did indeed constitute adequate evidence of "punishable aggression" as defined by the charter? (Unaforce itself could have no broad investigative or judicial powers if it were entrusted with invulnerable armament.)
   See answer on pages 105-9.

9. Why couldn't the responsibility for weighing such evidence and ordering Unaforce to impose a penalty be left to the "International Court of Justice" or any other arm of the present U.N.? And just what kind of "World Emergency Court" *could* safely be entrusted with it?
   See answer on pages 105-9.

10. Why would the three "Bloc Administrative Commissions" be needed? How would they function and be safeguarded?
   See answer on pages 109-12.

11. What are some of the *other* charter provisions that would be needed to make a Unaforce both effective and a good risk for all nations?
   See answer on pages 112-15.

12. When a badly "underdeveloped" nation repeatedly demonstrates it is not yet ready to govern itself wisely without outside help (and when a majority of its people *want* such

outside help on a strictly temporary basis), how could the Joint Bloc Administrative Commission protect such nation from exploiters and help it prepare itself for *good* self-government?
See answer on pages 115-18.

13. How can the *costs* of a Unaforce, of a World Emergency Court, and of the three Bloc Administrative Commissions be equitably distributed among all nations? And how reliably collected?
See answer on pages 118-19.

14. Just why would every nation be at least as safe from a militarily invulnerable Unaforce as was the U.S. from its own military establishment when *that* establishment had a world monopoly of the new mass weapons?
See answer on pages 119-22.

15. Why haven't the ideas that make this Unaforce plan worth intensive study by the world's best minds been published before now?
See answer on pages 123-24.

ANSWER TO QUESTION 1 (WHY CAN'T THE U.N. EVER BE TRUSTED WITH NUCLEAR WEAPONS?).

It has already been pointed out that (even if the U.N. charter were such that it *could* be trusted with nuclear weapons) the possession of such weapons still could not make the U.N. bluff-proof and therefore capable of enforcing anything. (Its diplomatic personnel and the whole city of New York could always be held hostage by a nuclear blackmailer to block enforcement.)

But some readers may still need to ask why no U.N.-controlled police force could ever be *trusted* with nuclear weapons. Here are two good reasons:

A. A nuclear-armed international police force can be adequately safeguarded against misuse of its power only if its charter can be so worded that it would be violating that charter if it took *any* really significant action not prescribed in detail by either the charter or a separate "World Emergency Court."

It will be shown elsewhere just why and how the responsibility and authority of a "Unaforce" *can* be that sharply limited. At this point, we need only show that the responsibilty and authority of the *U.N.* could *not* be that sharply limited except by destroying the U.N.'s present usefulness as a center of communication between nations. Many of the "domestic" affairs in which the U.N. has some degree of authority to intervene (civil wars, famines, boundary disputes, and so on) are so complex that no charter could possibly spell out *in advance* the precise action to be taken. Nor could the U.N. safely *wait* weeks or days or hours for a separate *court* to detail all action to be taken. The U.N. could not safely wait on the decisions of a separate court before using its nuclear weapons because (unlike a Unaforce) the U.N. can never be made invulnerable to successful attack.

B. Another reason that a U.N. police force could not be trusted with nuclear weapons is that, under the U.N. type of charter, a nation long avowedly dedicated to the goal of world conquest (the U.S.S.R.) has the right to *veto* any U.N. action aimed at *preventing* such conquest. Such a veto right could be used by a would-be conqueror to unduly influence the choice and behavior of U.N. police personnel. The only kind of international police force that *could* be trusted with nuclear weapons would be one whose charter is of a type to insure that at least a plurality of all its police personnel could always be controlled by those nations having the *most to lose* by any violation of the charter. Throughout history, a police force has proved of value to a society only when the selection and replacement of most of its policemen could be controlled by those *least likely to benefit* from "outlaw" police actions. Under the U.N. type of charter, a would-be world-conqueror could influence the selection and replacement of far too high a proportion of police personnel.

ANSWERS TO QUESTION 2 (WHY AND HOW CAN A "UNAFORCE" BE MADE TRULY INVULNERABLE TO SUCCESSFUL COUNTERATTACK AND THEREFORE *CAPABLE* OF ENFORCING ANTI-AGGRESSION LAWS WHEN GIVEN THE SAME WEAPONS THAT COULD

NOT MAKE THE U.N. OR ANY NATIONAL OR
WORLD "GOVERNMENT" INVULNERABLE?).

*A. Unaforce Would Have No "Non-expendable Possessions"
as the U.N. or Any National or World Government
Necessarily Does.*

Unaforce would have no big cities or industries of its own,
nothing which could be successfully threatened and held hostage
by a would-be breaker of the peace. The contract-suppliers of
Unaforce weapons, ammunition, food, uniforms, and so on would
be dispersed among the nations of all *three* Voting Blocs. Such
contract-suppliers could not themselves be held hostage to
immobilize Unaforce because none of them would "belong to"
Unaforce and the Unaforce charter would give Unaforce no
option to vacillate or yield to a blackmailer attempting to hold
such contract-suppliers hostage.

*B. Unaforce Weapons and Personnel Would Be Completely
Isolated from Any Really Tempting Targets for Mass Weapons.*

Unaforce submarine bases and other weapons installations
would be restricted to tiny remote islets all over the globe where
an attack on them could not threaten any important civilian
targets. And the Unaforce "Headquarters Staff" could also be
housed deep in the bowels of some remote island mountain,
where a threat to such staff could not threaten any big cities or
industries. With several hundred nuclear-armed submarines
roaming the seven seas for Unaforce, and with all of its installations completely divorced from blackmailable cities and industries, even the U.S. or the Soviet Union could not hope to cripple
Unaforce by a surprise first strike. And the absolute certainty of
intolerable retaliation *by* Unaforce would insure that no first
strike against Unaforce would ever be attempted.

*C. There Would Be an Immediate and Overwhelming
Superiority of Unaforce Arms.*

When today's two largest nuclear powers had reached

agreement on the wording of a Unaforce charter, there should be no great difficulty in getting the required two thirds of the other nations in *each* of the three Voting Blocs to ratify it. (Anything on which the U.S. and U.S.S.R. could fully agree would, after all, be a tremendous improvement for such other nations over the horrible hazards they would soon be facing without a Unaforce.) Once the charter was signed by two-thirds of the nations in each of the three Blocs, the necessary Unaforce personnel could probably be selected and trained and the necessary submarine bases and remote airfields built within perhaps one year.

Then, of course, would come the critical hours during which today's nuclear-armed nations would be transferring the bulk of their nuclear armed submarines and bombers to Unaforce. Just how could this initial transfer of weapons be effected with the least risk of some double-cross? Actually, *apart* from any bombers, as soon as trained Unaforce personnel were in possession of a hundred nuclear-armed submarines, the risk of any nation's attempting a double-cross would be too great to be tempting. Even without any help from other nations at the start, the Americans and Russians *alone* could quickly deliver these 100 submarines to Unaforce. Suppose a day and an hour were set when these two nations would each have fifty nuclear-armed subs at some huge but remote harbor for transfer to Unaforce. As it would be understood that each of the two nations could have only the same limited number of support ships in the area that day, the two forces would be too evenly balanced to warrant any last-minute double-crosses by either. If any serious breach of good faith were committed by either party to the transfer, the other party could call the whole thing off, and the world would be in no worse shape than at present. But assuming that the transfer of these initial weapons to Unaforce went smoothly, Unaforce would, in a matter of hours, be near enough to invulnerable to assume its full functions at once. Under those circumstances, even a possible "holdout" nation like Red China would no longer be tempted to test its strength against the new Unaforce.

Why should the Americans and Russians bear the brunt of

this cost of providing Unaforce with its first armament? Because only they would have such submarines on hand to deliver, and they would no longer have any need for them; because there is no other way they can protect themselves from each other; and because the existence of Unaforce could *save* these two nations infinitely more in future outlay than it could save for the unarmed or more lightly-armed nations. Nevertheless, as detailed further on, the less powerful nations would be required to supply immediately food, uniforms, island real estate, labor, and so on. Later, the total cost of Unaforce operation would be prorated among all the nations in proportion to the net income of each.

To insure that Unaforce military superiority never would be challenged by a possessor of some new technological discovery, the charter would enable Unaforce to contract for a continuous program of weapons *research* prorated among the three Voting Blocs.

D. No Worldwide, Continuous, On-the-Ground Arms-Inspection Program Would Be Needed.

As long as it was known by all and for certain that no attack against Unaforce had the remotest chance of success and that this invulnerable Unaforce had absolutely no option to vacillate in imposing specified penalties for specified types of aggression, there would be no need for any formal prohibition against a nation's arming itself. The utter futility of doing so under those circumstances would be so apparent that national armament would soon go out of style. Any nation that did long continue to build more national armament would be so conspicuous as to put the rest of the world on guard against voting with it on *any* Unaforce matter. Unaforce would, of course, have its own radar system for tracking all nuclear explosions, missile-launchings, and the like in order always to know instantly the geographical source of any attack. And the Unaforce engineering and pur-chasing staff would have access to the plants of all its authorized contract-suppliers. Furthermore, at least a plurality of all the world's diplomats, commercial travelers, commercial airlines, and so on will always be from nations strongly opposed to the schemes of a possible aggressor nation. Long before any potential aggressor could build and hide *enough* weapons of mass destruction to represent any serious threat, that nation (or those nations) would be under such concentrated world-suspicion that Unaforce would need no elaborate official inspection system to be fully on guard against surprise.

Another reason why no continuous official arms inspection program would be needed by Unaforce is that even if some mad dictator were silly enough to squander his nation's resources on an attempt to "out-arm" Unaforce, most of his own nationals would *not* be that silly. They would be certain to give Unaforce ample warning in order to protect their own families from the inevitable retribution their ruler was too dizzy to recognize as inevitable. When an international police force is so set up that even a full-scale nuclear attack on a completely surprise basis could not prevent the wiping out of the attacker a few hours later, there just isn't going to be any attack—or any attempt to get ready for an attack.

E. The Relationship Between Vacillation and Invulnerability Would Be Corrected.

One of the chief factors in the extreme vulnerability of all nations today is that they can and do vacillate about counter-attacking an aggressor in the early stages of his aggression. The anticipation of such vacillation is, of course, all the "invitation" needed by a brazen aggressor. If Peking and Moscow, for instance, now knew beyond all doubt that any preliminary aggression by them would *infallibly* result in penalties they could not accept, there might be no need for a Unaforce. But neither Washington nor Moscow is likely to take such an unequivocal position because of their terribly exposed "possessions." Both Moscow and Peking are recently reported to have committed acts against the other (border incidents) that, if persisted in, would result in prompt and intolerable penalties under a Unaforce.

Neither nation is now invulnerable to attack, partly because it can and does vacillate about imposing intolerable penalties. By contrast, Unaforce, with no "non-expendable" possessions to protect, can safely be bound by its charter to impose prescribed drastic penalties for specified acts of aggression *without* vacillation. It can therefore be made invulnerable, as a national "government" cannot be.

F. Even Unaforce Headquarters Could Not Be Held Hostage.

Because Unaforce would not be responsible for the *domestic* welfare of millions of people, as a national or big-city government is, and because it would not have to cope with the very complex problems that such responsibility entails, the total headquarters staff of Unaforce would be of very modest size and could be contained in less space than is required by the government of one major city. Its headquarters offices could therefore be buried deep in some remote island mountain. Even if, by some miracle, such a Unaforce headquarters were actually wiped out by an aggressor, that still could not save an aggressor from annihilation, because the officer in charge of each *individual* Unaforce weapon anywhere in the world would still be under oath to use it promptly against any fully identified attacker of Unaforce. (A few hours or even a few days delay in the accurate identification of the nation behind a sneak submarine or air attack on Unaforce could only postpone—not prevent—the annihilation of the attacking nation by surviving Unaforce submarines and bombers. As foreknowledge of the *inevitability* of such retribution would keep any competent military organization from attempting such a sneak attack in the first place, a Unaforce with the type of charter here outlined *could* be made invulnerable to military attack, as no nation or group of nations ever can be.

ANSWERS TO QUESTION 3 (WHY A UNAFORCE COULD NOT SERIOUSLY WRONG ANY NATION *WITHOUT* VIOLATING ITS CHARTER).

Whereas the U.S. or any other full-fledged "government" could greatly wrong its people *without* violating its basic constitution or charter, a Unaforce as here conceived could not do so. The difference is that any "government's" economic and other internal responsibilities are of such enormous complexity that no substantial part of its policy decisions could possibly be made for it in *advance* by its constitution. Because total Unaforce policy decisions would pertain only to a dozen or so anti-aggression laws, every facet of these laws could be embodied in the basic charter. If Unaforce radar showed unmistakably that nuclear missiles falling on nation *X* were originating in nation *Y*, Unaforce personnel would know from their charter precisely what they must do without consulting anyone. On the other hand, if the source of an attack appeared to be a group of unidentified submarines or if one nation were accusing another of mere threats of force, the evidence would be weighed and the decision made by the World Emergency Court. In either case, the men "at the triggers" of the Unaforce weapons would not be making policy decisions and could hardly wrong any nation seriously without violating their charter. It should, by the way, be noted that the hypothetical case in which nuclear missiles were raining down on some nation just would not happen with a Unaforce on the job. The kind of *odds* against the success of any such aggression, which would be posted by the Unaforce charter, would insure that no such attack on any substantial scale would ever occur. Any such attack would represent deliberate suicide by the attacker. Another thing to remember at this point is that when eventual retribution is absolutely *certain,* nobody is tempted to commit aggression just because he might be able to conceal his identity for a few hours or days. With a Unaforce in effect, the world could *afford* the luxury of careful court hearings before allowing Unaforce to impose the charter penalties.

ANSWER TO QUESTION 4 (WHY AND HOW A MILITARILY INVULNERABLE UNAFORCE CAN BE KEPT FROM VIOLATING ITS CHARTER AND BECOMING

THE PRIVATE TOOL OF SOME AGGRESSION-
MINDED NATION).

*A. It Would Have a High Degree of "Automatic" Security
from Takeover.*

Before trying to decide just what special charter provisions
are needed to help safeguard Unaforce from subversion, we
should recognize that it would have a very high degree of built-in,
automatic security from takeover. No straight-thinking national
government would ever *want* to steal full control of Unaforce
because (in addition to throwing away the great security Unaforce had been giving it) it would find Unaforce an almost
useless tool in private hands. For instance, let's say the Germans
(or Russians), after agreeing to the Unaforce charter and
actually experiencing the complete freedom from fear of mass
annihilation which Unaforce would be giving them, should,
incredibly, decide they would like to trade all that security for
another crack at world conquest. Assume further that such a
nation had actually been able to steal full control of Unaforce
and make it their private tool. The minute that happened, Unaforce would automatically *lose* the invulnerability that had made
it so effective. As the private tool of one (or a few) nations,
Unaforce would be of little more value to its new master than is
such a nation's *present* nuclear armament. The key cities of any
nation that had stolen control of Unaforce could again successfully be held hostage to immobilize the Unaforce weapons, as
their present weapons are immobilized by their possessions. Any
stealer and misuser of Unaforce would soon have thousands of
clever and hate-maddened (but possessionless and unidentifiable)
individuals able and anxious to smuggle mass annihilation into its
home cities. The threat they posed would be far too genuine for
Unaforce's new master to ignore. With that prospect, no halfway
sane government would ever *want* to sacrifice its complete
security under Unaforce by trying to steal full control of
Unaforce. But as there will always be a few madmen around, we
come to the next point.

B. The Right Patterns of Voting Control, of Personnel Selection, and of Checks and Balances Could Almost Surely Eliminate Any Remaining Risk of Successful Subversion.

The organization chart on a preceding page summarizes the proposed make-up of each of the world's three Voting Bloc's. But just how and why can this particular grouping of nations insure that at least a plurality of all Unaforce officers and men would *always* be strongly opposed to any violation of the Unaforce charter? As already demonstrated, Unaforce could not seriously wrong any nation without violating its own charter because the extreme simplicity of Unaforce duties and authority permit the charter itself—with occasional interpretation by the World Emergency Court—to predetermine all of Unaforce's more significant actions. As Unaforce would have no responsibility for any of the complex *domestic* problems of nations, the only susbstantial reason any nation could have for wanting the charter violated would be an urge to join (and become a pawn of) some nation bent on world conquest.

The problem, then, in deciding the composition of the three Voting Blocs is simply to make sure that at least a plurality of the nations in each of *two* of these Blocs is of the type that value their own independence more than any "vassal's share" of attempted world conquest. A plurality of the nations herein assigned to Blocs B and C would (as demonstrated in these pages) *always* fit that description:

Composition of Bloc A

Recent history pretty well determines this first grouping for us. The only nations presently showing any interest in world conquest are the Communist nations. They all belong together in Bloc A. As at least two-thirds of the separate national entities in the Communist group are oriented toward Moscow, it can be assumed that (for the present at least) Bloc A's single vote would be controlled by the Kremlin.

Composition of Bloc B

The only other group of nations having the kind of economic and military base needed to launch an attempt at world conquest —the only other group that, by any stretch of the imagination, could ever initiate an attempt at world conquest and therefore want the charter violated—is that group listed as Bloc B. This Bloc would consist of those "Free World" nations that have a high level of literacy and industrial prosperity and *in which the vote of "the masses" can greatly influence their governmental policies.* The U.S., Canada, most of Western Europe, Japan, Australia, Israel, and so on would fit this description. Since these nations were *voluntarily disbanding* their empires at a time when one of them had a world monopoly of atomic weapons, it is hardly conceivable that, with a Unaforce in operation, two thirds of them would ever again be even remotely interested in attempting to rebuild such empires. Nevertheless, since they do have the economic and military power, they are the group (if any) against which Bloc A would need protection.

Composition of Bloc C

Since the "Great Power" Blocs (A and B) are largely responsible for the threat of annihilation that now hangs over the human race—a threat which can be ended only by giving these two Blocs full protection from each *other*—the "balance of power" between them must be held by a third Voting Bloc. This Bloc C must be so constituted that at least two thirds of its member nations could not conceivably ever *want* the charter violated. The obvious choice of nations for such a Bloc C would be those which have neither great military power nor the literacy level and industrial base on which to build such military power—in short, all of the world's nations who have always been helpless pawns in the struggles between the Great Powers. These nations, above all others, can appreciate the true value of freedom and of the reliable protection from exploitation that only a Unaforce can give them. If, after once experiencing under a Unaforce real security from all "foreign devils," such nations as Burma, Iran, the Congo, Paraguay, Indonesia, Morocco, Cambodia, or Nigeria were to conspire with any would-be world conqueror to make Unaforce violate its charter, they would not only be throwing away the only real security they had ever known but would get in exchange for such sacrifice only the same kind of "pawn" status they had before Unaforce was created. They just would not do it.

It will of course be pointed out that some of the 80 or more nations who would wield Bloc C's one vote are so unstable emotionally or have such dizzy dictators that they could easily be *misled* as to what is actually in their own best long-term interest. This is doubtless true for a few of them, but not for two thirds of them. The demonstrable fact is that *today's would-be* world conquerors (the Communists) are finding most "primitive" peoples much harder to fool, where their freedom is concerned, than are some of the industrial world's pampered intellectuals. Only those who have personally suffered from a serious *lack* of freedom can fully understand its importance. The more emotional a nation is, the greater the importance to it of the "right of self-determination." Again and again, the "underdeveloped" nations, when forced to choose between more economic or military aid and their right to govern themselves, have sacrificed material gain to preserve their precious freedom. They are the best possible repository for the deciding vote as to whether or not Unaforce should violate its charter. As long as the Bloc B and Bloc C votes were cast for Unaforce personnel dedicated to the integrity of the charter, it could not be successfully subverted.

Well, then, how is that the Cubans so readily exchanged a ruthless but "local" dictator for one controlled by foreign Communists. That is not by any stretch of the imagination a typical example. The Cuban people could be so deceived by would-be world conquerors only because they believed—and had every right to believe—that the U.S. Monroe Doctrine would always protect them from any "overseas" conspirators and because the U.S. State Department blindly endorsed Castro to them as a mere local reformer.

Then how about the chance that some of the highly emotional Arab rulers might let a would-be world conqueror talk them into helping subvert Unaforce in order to have a chance to pay off their ancient grudge against Israel? Possible, but not likely. In any case, the Arabs all together would have little influence on the nature of the Bloc C vote. At present, the Arabs doubtless fear *further* heavy losses of territory to Israel, which could cause them to take some of the wild risks they are now taking. But with a Unaforce in operation, the Arabs could have nothing *further* to fear from anybody, as long as the charter was not violated. And even such excitable people as they would not be likely to risk losing the only security they had ever known just to pay off comparatively minor *past* grudges.

C. The Sheer Size of Bloc C Would Be an Important Safety Factor.

Assuming that, eventually, a very few of the 80 or so nations in Bloc C, or their rulers, could be successfully brainwashed or bribed by some would-be aggressor, this large *number* of nations in Bloc C would still make it a safe balance-wheel. Even *without* much present protection from veiled Communist threats, at least 95% of all the nations that would be in Bloc C have steadfastly refused to exchange their freedom for the tempting baits being dangled before them by the Communists. *With* a Unaforce in effect to fully protect them from such threats, it is utterly inconceivable that as many as two thirds of these 80 or so nations would ever vote for Unaforce personnel suspected of favoring charter violation or fail to vote for prompt impeachment of such personnel. And unless most of Bloc C's third of Unaforce personnel *could* be talked into helping violate the charter, the only way a very dangerous proportion of the total Unaforce staff could be subverted would be by collusion between "capitalist" Bloc B and Communist Bloc A. But if Blocs B and A *both* wanted the same thing badly enough they would work toward amendment rather than violation. Bloc A and B nations are not *now* attempting any *joint* exploitation of the nations that would be in

Bloc C, and under a Unaforce, they would have even *less* reason or opportunity to do so.

D. *Voting Rules Would Help Guard Against Charter Violation.*

Each of the three *Blocs* of nations would have one single vote, the nature of which would be determined by two-thirds of all the nations in that Bloc.

All three of these "Bloc Votes" would be necessary for the adoption or later amendment of the charter itself.

Two of these Bloc Votes would be required to elect a member of the Unaforce High Command. After the first ten years of Unaforce existence, its three top officers would be elected only from among *experienced* Unaforce staff, and all three of these top officers would from the start have to be from *different* Blocs, so that the High Command could never be "packed" to favor any one Bloc.

Each Bloc's five members on the World Emergency Court and its nine-member Administrative Commission would be elected by that Bloc's "Heads of State" by a two-thirds plurality.

Each Bloc would "nominate" its own one-third of the total candidates for the Unaforce staff through its Administrative Commission. But it would be useless for any Block Commission to nominate any candidate whose detailed life-record failed to meet the extremely stiff standards of character, emotional stability, experience, and education set forth by the charter. Such a nominee could be rejected by the Unaforce High Command, a plurality of which would always be representative of Blocs *other* than the one offering this particular nominee. And if, after the actual appointment of a given nominee to the Unaforce staff, he was suspected of conspiracy to violate the charter, he could be arrested and brought to trial by *either* the Unaforce command or by a two-thirds vote of the three Bloc Commissions.

Also by a two-thirds vote, the three Bloc Commissions could veto any major purchase contract placed by Unaforce.

Any evidence of "punishable aggression" that was not, on the face of it, unmistakably valid would be subject to a World

Emergency Court ruling before Uniforce could impose its pre-scribed penalities. An example of "unmistakably valid evidence" would be a case in which the Unaforce radar system showed beyond all doubt that a number of nuclear missiles falling on Unaforce installations were being launched from nation X. In such a case, Unaforce would have no choice but to impose the charter-prescribed penalties on nation X.

E. The Effect of Changing World Conditions on This "Balance of Power" Would be Considered.

As previously indicated, the charter would have to contain some such provisions as the following:

1. Any Bloc C or Bloc B nation that later changed to a Communist form of government (most unlikely) would thereby automatically be transferred to Bloc A.

2. No "historically" Bloc A or B nation could *ever* change to Bloc C.

3. If, as the years passed, any Bloc C or Bloc A nation felt qualified for transfer to Bloc B, it would have that right *only* with the unanimous approval of all the nations already in Bloc B.

4. If and when all but *nine* Bloc C nations should attain a really high level of literacy, industrialization, and affluence and be admitted to one of the other Blocs, these nine remaining nations would become *permanent* members of Bloc C. This position would be no affront to them because their Bloc would still hold the "balance of power" between the other two Blocs, and these remaining nations in Bloc C would still be the ones that *most* needed the protection of a faithful Unaforce. If, how-ever, any of these last nine nations in Bloc C should ever adopt a Communist government (and therefore be *forced* to transfer to Bloc A), then the last *previous* transferee from Bloc C to B would automatically be returned to Bloc C to maintain that Bloc's usefulness as a balance.

F. There Would Be a System of Checks and Balances.

As is the case with the U.S. Constitution, the Unaforce

charter would contain provisions to enable the Bloc Administrative Commissions, the World Emergency Court, and the Unaforce High Command to keep an eye on each other's actions and help to "keep each other honest." For example:

1. Any attempt by the fully identified agent of a given nation to influence by bribery or threat of force any member of the World Emergency Court would enable the Court, by a plurality vote, to order the destruction of the capitol city of such nation. (Such a penalty would be carried out of course, only after charter-prescribed warnings had been issued and ignored.) The same action could be instituted directly, at the *option* of Unaforce, on a "simple majority" finding of the court. Any individual who could *not* be surely identified as the agent of a particular nation but who attempted to bribe or threaten a Court Justice would be subject to the death penalty, on a majority finding of the court. Any nation which disclaimed such an agent could hardly dare to object to his being extradited for punishment. Similarly, any attempt to influence by bribery or threat of force any member of a Bloc Administrative Commission would be subject to the same penalty.

2. No one could be appointed to the Unaforce staff except when rigidly screened against very stiff charter specifications by one of the Bloc Commissions. But neither could one of these Bloc Commissions put anyone on the Unaforce staff without the final approval of the Governor-General and one of his two key aides.

3. Although the three members of the Unaforce High Command would be elected (for "staggered" ten-year terms) directly by a plurality of the three "Bloc Votes," i.e., directly by the Heads of State of the various nations, the nominees for these three top Unaforce posts would (after the initial ten years of Unaforce operation) all be seasoned Unaforce officers *originally* screened and nominated by one or another of the Bloc Administrative Commissions. As the charter would require that the Governor-General and his two top aides must be from *different* Blocs, no one Bloc could ever fully dominate the High Command.

4. Any Unaforce officer suspected of attempting or plotting charter violation who was *not* promptly detected, removed from

Unaforce premises, and put on trial by his *own* High Command could be so arrested and tried by the Court, on orders from any two of the Bloc Administrative Commissions. Conversely, any two of the top Unaforce officers could order the arrest and trial of any Administrative Commission member suspected of plotting charter violation or other misconduct in office.

5. Any member of the World Emergency Court suspected of accepting bribes or otherwise violating his oath of office could be temporarily disqualified by a plurality of the three Bloc Commissions or by a plurality of the High Command, subject to final impeachment or reinstatement by a plurality of the Heads of State in *two* of the Voting Blocs.

6. The High Command (with its own technical staff) would initiate purchase contracts for its necessary weapons, uniforms, and so on, but any of its "major" contracts would be subject to veto by a plurality of the three Bloc Administrative Commissions.

G. Another Safeguard Against Subversion of Unaforce Would Be the Contract-Purchasing System for Unaforce Weapons.

Assuming that not more than one Voting Bloc would (by the necessary two-thirds vote of its members) ever favor any given attempt to subvert Unaforce and that at least half of the contract-suppliers of nuclear weaons to Unaforce would always be in the *other* two Blocs, it should be obvious that, although any weapons a given supplier might have on hand could not be used effectively against Unaforce itself, they *could* be used with terrible effectiveness against the cities and industries of any nation that had just stolen control of Unaforce. Foreknowledge of this fact by any would-be aggressor would provide an extremely powerful additional safeguard against attempted subversion of Unaforce. Since the nation in which such weapons had been produced would also have cities vulnerable to the aggressor's mass weapons, the danger to an illegal owner of Unaforce would come not so much from the governments of *nations* holding weapons for delivery to Unaforce as from groups of unidentifiable private individuals who could steal such weapons and smuggle them into the cities of the aggressor nation before it could bring its newly captured Unaforce fully to bear.

At this point, let's try to visualize in a little more detail the predicament of "Nation X," if and when it had succeeded in brainwashing, bribing, or frightening part of the Unaforce staff into betraying their trust and becoming tools of Nation X. Ensuing developments could be somewhat as follows:

1. Shortly after gaining control of the Unaforce staff (and slaughtering that two-thirds or more of the staff that had remained loyal to the charter), the rulers of Nation X might find in their morning mail an "untraceable" note, lettered in their own language and postmarked in their own capitol city, saying: "Weapons of mass destruction are now secreted in each of your key cities. They will be used to wipe all those cities off the map if you persist in forcing Unaforce to violate its charter and fail to return control of it to the three Voting Blocs."

2. It would be useless for Nation X to order Unaforce to destroy the senders of the blackmail letter, because they might be nationals of any one of 50 or 100 different nations. As Unaforce mass weapons would be of no value except against mass targets like great cities and industries, Nation X could hardly order the destruction of all the thousands of cities from which the blackmailers might have come or in which they might be hidden.

3. The new masters of Unaforce would have two choices: they could either call off their conquest and restore Unaforce, or they could risk annihilation of their home cities by merely augmenting their secret police forces, searching every corner of every building in each of their key cities, and conducting a reign of terror among their own nationals to find clues to the blackmailer's identity. Having gone thus far, they would of course choose the latter course of action.

4. But this would net them nothing. At the end of several months, they would have found no hidden weapons, because there were none to find—*that* time around. So the people of Nation X are again allowed to enter and leave their cities (under certain circumstances), and they breathe a little easier.

5. But now the individual conspirators who had sent the "phony" blackmail letter conclude that Nation *X* will not liberate Unaforce without some real *action*. They gradually filter their men back into Nation *X*, along with poison for the water supply, or a bottle of new plague germs, or the components of nuclear bombs, and proceed (over a period of a year or two perhaps) to secrete such weapons in each of Nation *X*'s key cities. But this time, they don't bother to warn their victim (who has already had fair warning). They simply proceed to exterminate several hundred million Nation *X*'s people, along with its key industries and most of the ruling hierarchy. After that, no nation would ever again be likely to attempt world conquest.

6. But to pursue the hypothesis to its ultimate conclusion, let's say that several members of the ruling clique of Nation *X* happened to be traveling at the time their home office and home cities were wiped out and that these brave men still refused to take the hint. Instead they merely moved their capitol to some other part of the world and started over again. A few years later, this new "World Capitol" would also be wiped out by a handful of individual smugglers—and so on, *ad infinitum*.

7. Eventually the nation that had performed the incredible miracle of stealing full control of Unaforce would become very sorry indeed that it had done so. In short, a *captive* Unaforce would be about as useless to its captors as the present U.N. would be. Foreknowledge of these possibilities should prevent any nation from even wanting to steal Unaforce.

H. A Faithful Unaforce Could Protect All Nations Even from Undercover, Individual Smugglers of Mass Weapons.

Actually, the only real security from outraged *individual* purveyors of mass annihilation that any government can ever *again* hope to have lies in its reasonably just treatment of the people it governs. A Unaforce can fully protect each nation from all other *nations;* but the only way it can protect a government from groups of private individuals whom it has grievously wronged would be by making it *unnecessary* for any nation to hold its political dissidents in captivity. For instance, it is extremely unlikely that any group of individuals with the high level of mental and emotional capacity needed to organize the annihilation of a great city or group of cities would ever have a deep enough grudge against the governments of Switzerland, Denmark, England, or the U.S., to deliberately wipe out tens of millions of their fellow citizens just to punish the *governments* of those countries. On the other hand, it isn't at all hard to conceive that perfectly sane and competent Czechs, East Germans, Poles, or Hungarians could bring themselves to wipe out the whole populations of Moscow and Leningrad *if* they came to the conclusion that no *other* course of action could ever free their children and grandchildren from what they consider a brutal and tyranical captivity. To restate the case, when a citizen does not approve of his government *but is free to leave and take his family and at least part of his possessions with him* (as in the U.S., Holland, or Japan), that man (if he is sane enough to be really dangerous with mass weapons) just does not build up enough of a "head of steam" to consider destroying millions of his fellow men to pay off *past* grudges. Only when he feels *permanently and hopelessly trapped* might a dangerous caliber of man consider doing so. With a Unaforce in operation to fully protect them from all foreign plots, the Communist governments could for the first time in their history "afford" to export all their most violent dissidents and their families, thus relieving the extreme emotional pressure on these dissidents and very sharply lessening their temptation to avenge *old* wrongs by wiping out whole populations. In this indirect way, a Unaforce could provide all nations with almost complete protection from even *individual* smugglers of mass weapons.

I. The Odds Would Be High Against Subverting Unaforce by Brainwashing or Bribery.

Unaforce personnel (especially the top officials) would be extremely hard to brainwash or bribe, because:

1. *Far More Carefully Screened Than Any Other Military*

Force in History. Before anyone could become a nominee for appointment or election to the Unaforce staff, he would have to meet charter specifications of unprecedented severity. The charter would require that, for even the bottom jobs on the Unaforce staff, the candidate would have to be a technically trained college graduate with a lifetime record of character, emotional stability, courage, and past military, police, or technical *responsibility*, as well as experience.

2. *Unprecedented Pay Levels and Prestige.* Because Unaforce would need no large masses of infantry and because the total cost of Unaforce would be so trivial compared to the *present* military costs of of the world's nations, the world could afford to pay even the lowest echelon of Unaforce manpower handsomely, at rates currently being paid to junior executives in the more advanced countries. Even those on the bottom rung of the Una-force ladder would indeed *be* junior executives, working with advanced technological developments. The pay and fringe bene-fits of the four top Unaforce officials should make them among the world's very best paid "public servants" (at least on a par with the pay of any national President or Prime Minister). The three top Unaforce officials would be wielding more power than any other individuals in the world and should be paid accordingly. Such compensation, plus the extraordinary care with which they were screened before appointment, plus the satisfaction and enormous *prestige* of exercising the greatest power in the world, would leave such men little reason to be tempted by bribes. Furthermore, men of the very high caliber who could meet the charter specifications and who were making a life-career of Unaforce service would soon develop an *esprit de corps*—a pride in the noble principles behind the Unaforce charter—that would insure that any whisper of betrayal would be echoed to the Bloc Administrative Commissions long before it could become a great hazard.

3. *The Usual "Tools of Subversion" Not Useful Against Unaforce.* One of the very best assurances that at least a plurality of Unaforce personnel could never be "brainwashed" into betray-ing their charter lies in the fact that Unaforce could never be

charged with "shameful failure" to provide better housing for the poor, to lower taxation, to educate the uneducable, or to abolish crime in the streets. Demagogues in the past have always relied *chiefly* on such charges to turn the army against its government. But no such charges could ever be leveled against Unaforce, and no Unaforce officer could ever be convinced that his family and friends at home were being wronged by strict Unaforce adherence to its charter. Any "world-government" *will* eventually be undermined and overthrown because it has failed to solve economic or other domestic problems. But precisely because Unaforce would *not* be a world government and could therefore never be charged with failure to solve "insoluble" problems, its personnel would never be easy targets for those who would sway them from their duty.

4. *Triple-Check on All Nominees to Unaforce Staff.* Six months before submitting to the Unaforce High Command any candidate for appointment to its staff, the Bloc Administrative Commission of that Bloc would submit to all the Heads of State in that Bloc the fully documented lifetime record of such candidate. Thus each nation in that Bloc would have ample opportunity to double-check any of its own Commission's choices before they were submitted for High Command approval.

5. *Safety of Letting Bloc C Make Some of Its Appointments from "Other Blocs."* Since many of the Unaforce personnel would have to be highly trained and experienced technologists and industrial technicians and since, at first anyway, Bloc C might have difficulty supplying from among its *own* nationals its full one-third share of such experts who could pass the charter's stringent specifications, Bloc C might need to choose a few such appointees from one of the other Blocs. And since the Communist Bloc would then be in no position to *threaten* the Bloc C nations into choosing a Communist appointee, Bloc C would almost certainly turn to Bloc B for such temporary help in filling their quota of Unaforce technicians. (Nearly all the defenseless nations here assigned to Bloc C have recently made it quite clear that *only* brute force could make them accept Communist control of their lives.)

6. *The Great Preponderance of Unaforce Personnel Opposing Any Violation of the Charter.* With the possible exception just mentioned, the national origin of all Unaforce personnel would be prorated among the three Voting Blocs, so that two-thirds of the total staff would always be from Blocs *other* than the one which might be involved in any subversive conspiracy. In addition to this "safe" two-thirds of the staff, there would almost certainly be many Unaforce men from the Bloc *involved* in such a conspiracy whose native good sense and/or loyalty to an organization they had learned to love and respect would more than balance any loyalty they might have to a homeland bent on attempted conquest against hopeless odds. But with even two thirds of all Unaforce men loyally standing guard over the defectors, the charter would not be in great danger of violation—not when the loyal two thirds or more were under oath to instantly arrest (or if necessary, kill) any minority of their fellows involved in subversive activities.

ANSWERS TO QUESTION 5 (WHY SOME POWER-MAD UNAFORCE OFFICER COULD NOT PERSONALLY SEIZE CONTROL AND USE UNAFORCE TO MAKE HIMSELF WORLD DICTATOR).

A. Traditional Methods Would Fail.

Such power-grabbers as Hitler, Peron, Castro, and Nasser were able to get the support of an army in taking over a government primarily by pointing to the results of that government's allegedly bad policies and decisions. By blaming the established government for unemployment, poor educational facilities, high taxes, and civil strife, such demagogues were able to get the army's support for a coup. But such appeals would have no impact on the Unaforce staff because everyone would be fully aware that Unaforce had no power to make any decisions or formulate any policies regarding the domestic affairs of any nation, except by *violating* its charter. So, even if a suddenly demented Governor-General of Unaforce attempted to use this most potent of all the traditional "tools of subversion," he could only make himself ridiculous and get himself promptly arrested.

What, then, *might* a power-mad Unaforce officer actually attempt to do to get support for a personal *putsch?* Bribe his men? Brainwash them? Demagogues have often found it fairly easy to "mislead" or bribe a sizable proportion of the officers in their army, because the ordinary national army cannot afford to screen its recruits carefully enough and pay them well enough to get all *top-caliber* men. But the provisions of the Unaforce charter would insure that only a superb *quality* of men could ever be appointed to the Unaforce staff; and since they would *already* be by far the world's best paid and most honored men in their profession (as well as being of exceptional character and discernment), practically all of them would be very difficult indeed to mislead or bribe. Would many men of such top caliber actually consider exchanging their top pay, prestige, and self-respect for an alleged opportunity to "get rich quick" by helping a traitor meddle in the domestic affairs of troubled national governments? Doing so could only risk their lives and the lives of their loved ones and earn them the hatred and contempt of most of the world's people. So even deception and bribery would not be of great help to a would-be subverter of Unaforce—as they might be to those attempting the betrayal of a mere nation.

B. *Little Chance Would Exist for Appealing to Hurt Pride.*

Resentment over some personal *humiliation* has probably always been at the root of more betrayals of trust by *Key* officials than has mere greed for riches or power. Men like Hitler get their early support (and their key conspirators) from among those, who like themselves, feel "left out" or downtrodden. Unaforce charter specifications would insure that such resentful misfits would be spotted and elminated before they could be appointed to the Unaforce staff. Nevertheless, the charter should protect all Unaforce officers in every possible way from unnecessary personal *humiliation*. It should, for instance, provide that any key officer whose performance proved to be so inadequate as to necessitate a demotion (or who failed to win re-election to one of the High Command posts before he reached mandatory retirement age) would be retired rather than demoted—on full pension unless his conduct merited dishonorable discharge. In this way, Unaforce officers would be highly insulated from the desire for revenge that powers most subversive conspiracies.

C. At Least Two Thirds of His Officers and Men Would Always Be Against His Attempted Power-Grab.

If even a Governor-General of Unaforce should become so demented as to attempt a personal power-grab, he could make no very dangerous progress without the support of at least half of his key officers and men. But the foregoing voting-control pattern would insure that at least two thirds of all his officers and men would always be from backgrounds and represent interests *other* than those of the conspirators. Unlike the men in any national army, no large proportion of the Unaforce staff could ever be "reached" by the same type of appeals. Any Governor-General's second and third in command would always have been elected independently of him, and each would always have an entirely different set of interests and problems in his homeland. They could not all conceivably go mad at the same time; and unless they did, two thirds of them at least would always oppose a personal putsch by one of them. And each would be under oath to instantly arrest and remove from Unaforce premises any superior who even hinted at conspiring to violate the charter.

D. Unaforce Men Would Be Safeguarded Against Personal Blackmail.

The kind of personal blackmail widely used today by the secret agents of one nation to control and subvert another nation's government employees would be far less effective where Unaforce personnel was concerned. Whereas in the ordinary national government politicians or scientists with blackmailable personal vices or other past mistakes often get into high office without any really exhaustive screening, even the lowest echelons of the Unaforce staff would have to have personal histories that could be triply certified as "blackmail-proof." Such certification would be by the skilled investigative staffs of the three different Bloc Administrative Commissions—each of which would be competing with the other two to uncover any blackmailable facts in the background of another Bloc's nominees.

E. Violation of Charter Would Sacrifice Unaforce's Invulnerability to Counterattack.

If a group of Unaforce officers ever did succeed in using Unaforce weapons to take over direct control of great cities and industries, they would thereby rob Unaforce and themselves of invulnerability to successful blackmail threats. Smugglers of mass weapons (stolen from some of the various contract suppliers of such weapons) could destroy stolen industries almost as fast as crooked Unaforce officials could lay claim to them. And the foreknowledge of this result would cause any subversive group to think twice before even trying to take over private control of Unaforce.

All in all, any Unaforce official would *have* to be a madman to even consider trying to use Unaforce in a plot to take over world control. And men of the caliber required by the Unaforce charter just don't become followers of madmen. Any such mad conspirator would be surrounded by thousands of able "loyalists" ready to arrest or shoot him down if he betrayed his trust. What Unaforce official who was *not* mentally and emotionally unhinged would deliberately exchange so much of the world's respect and rewards for so much of the world's contempt and an almost certain traitor's death?

ANSWERS TO QUESTION 6 (WHY THE "GREAT POWERS" IN BLOCS A AND B CAN NEVER PROTECT THEMSELVES FROM EACH *OTHER,* EXCEPT BY GIVING THE WORLD'S THIRD VOTE TO A BLOC COMPOSED OF THE "UNDERDEVELOPED" AND DEFENSELESS NATIONS. AND HOW SUCH "HUNGRY"

BLOC C NATIONS CAN BE PREVENTED FROM
TAKING SERIOUS ADVANTAGE OF THE TWO MORE
PROSPEROUS BLOCS).

To satisfy ourselves that the single Bloc C vote would be
safest in the hands of the 80 of so "least developed" nations, we
need to recheck the steps used in arriving at this conclusion, as
follows:

A. Without violating its charter, Unaforce could not meddle
in the domestic affairs of any nation or even punish one nation
for offenses against another except as agreed on in advance by all
three Blocs and precisely authorized by the charter.

B. The only sufficient reason any nation could have for
wanting that kind of Unaforce to violate its charter would be
that such nation was bent on world conquest. But the only type
of nation which could have the faintest chance of succeeding as
a world conqueror would be one having the high levels of literacy
and economic development needed to create and direct a modern
war machine. Since the nations herein assigned to Blocs A and
B do have technological and economic potential, either one of
these two Blocs could, conceivably, attempt such world conquest.
And the world's most desperate problems today stem directly
from the need of these two Blocs for protection from each *other*.

C. But neither Bloc A nor Bloc B can ever accomplish this
solely by its *own* diplomatic or military prowess, because each
possesses vast industries and cities that can be "held hostage" by
the other.

D. The kind of Bloc C that could best protect the two "Great
Power" Blocs from each other would consist of those nations that
do *not* themselves have the modern industrial base essential to
any serious attempt at world conquest. If such "defenseless"
nations in Bloc C could not hope to launch a successful world
conquest they would indeed have nothing to gain and everything
to lose by any violation of the Unaforce charter. Hence they
would be the safest possible repository for the world's "balance of
power" vote regarding selection and removal of Unaforce
personnel.

E. "Not so fast," says someone. "Even though nations like

Egypt, Syria, India, Haiti, Niger, and Argentina would certainly not want the Unaforce charter violated in order to attempt world conquest 'on their own,' could not the rulers of some of these nations be bribed or brainwashed into *supporting* some reckless Great Power in such an attempt?" The current evidence seems very clear that few indeed of them could be so tricked. For some years now Moscow and Peking, for instance, have been using thinly veiled threats as well as every propaganda trick in the book to make all underdeveloped countries adopt Communist governments, which would make them subservient to Moscow or Peking. Surely, many of these economically and militarily weak nations have been "playing footsie" with the Communist nations to gain some economic aid or to avoid terrorism by Communist infiltrators; but the fact remains that *almost none* of them have yielded to these great pressures and actually adopted Communist-type governments. It is not as strange as it sounds that the simplest and most mercurial peoples of the earth are actually the ones hardest to fool where their "right of self-determination" is concerned. They have not had long years of luxurious freedom in which to *forget* the hard realities of vassaldom. They have not lost the gut-instinct for freedom of choice. They haven't had the chance too many Western intellectuals have had to *forget* the pain and humiliation of being pushed around by some insolent "big brother." They know all too well from fairly recent hard experience what it is *like* to be without freedom.

If these underdeveloped and militarily defenseless nations, even when exposed to current relentless pressures, are not now being fooled or frightened into chaining themselves to the juggernaut of a world conqueror, why on earth should anyone fear that many of them would do so *after* a Unaforce was giving them absolute protection from such external pressures? If such Bloc C nations don't want to become vassal states under some would-be world conqueror, they would have no reason to want the Unaforce charter violated. And if its charter were not violated, Unaforce could not seriously harm any nation. Thus the least-developed nations plus the non-Communist dictatorships make up the best possible bet for the third Voting Bloc which would exercise the world's third and decisive vote in matters concerning Unaforce.

Remember that each of Bloc C's nominees to the Unaforce staff would have to be approved by the Unaforce High Command, and remember that a plurality of the High Command would, by charter requirement, always be from nations *other* than those of a particular nominating Bloc.

And lastly, don't forget that each member of the Bloc C Administrative Commission (which selected Bloc C nominees to the Unaforce staff) would be elected by a *plurality* of all the 80 or so nations in that Bloc. Thus, even if as many as a dozen or so of these Bloc C nations should prove dizzy enough to participate in a plot to violate the charter, their influence on the choice of their Bloc's Commissioners and of their Bloc's nominees to Unaforce would be *nil*. A plurality of the nations here assigned to Bloc C could always be depended on to choose Unaforce nominees dedicated to an inviolate Unaforce charter.

F. Could "Nonwhite" Nations in Bloc C Ever Use Their Bloc Vote to Promote "Race War"?

Suppose the nonwhite nations in Communist Bloc A could gain the necessary two-thirds control of their Bloc's vote and then persuade all the nonwhite nations in Bloc C to join them. Could they then make Unaforce a tool for a "holy war" based on skin color? Not when all such nonwhite nations were fully protected from any future white "empire builder" by a Unaforce faithfully adhering to its charter. What could a race war possibly gain for most nonwhite nations to anywhere near offset what they would surely *lose* by any subversion of Unaforce?

Does anyone really think the nonwhite Japanese, Malaysians, Thais, Pakistanis, Abyssinians, and Ethiopians, would throw away complete security from foreign oppressors under a faithful Unaforce to put themselves at the mercy of some nonwhite "master" with empire-building ambitions like the Red Chinese? Neither skin color nor raw greed can ever weigh that heavily against a nation's desire for the permanently *protected* right to rule itself in its own way. In yesterday's world, this might not have been true; but in today's world, the nonwhite "have-not" nations have little reason to complain of unfair treatment. And in tomorrow's world (under a proper Unaforce charter), any nonwhite nation's complete security from foreign threats and from nuclear annihilation would far outweigh any possible long-term gains the nonwhite nations could hope to make by a fanatic race war.

Under a Unaforce, the white industrial nations would be able and anxious to sharply step up the hundreds of billions in aid funds they are already giving to the "have-not" nations, because doing so would sharply increase the size of their world market. Any outright robbery scheme by the "have-not" nations based on color of skin could only kill the goose that is now laying these golden eggs in their lap. Many rulers of nations that would be in Bloc C are already fully aware that the true wealth of the white industrial nations is not something which can be trucked away in a quick raid. They realize it is, rather, the *continuing* production capacity of an ambitious and technologically-trained people equipped with proper tools. And many of these rulers are, unquestionably, already aware that stealing the basic tools of white industrial nations could not benefit them as much as can the educational and pump-priming aid *willingly* given them by white nations whose productive capacity is unimpaired.

An interesting sidelight on the relative unimportance of purely racial factors in today's world is noticeable in the U.S. right now. In spite of the current (and long overdue) racial confrontation in the U.S., most of even the wildest black agitators make it very clear that they feel they have a lot more in common with white America than with black Africa. Very few of the militant U.S. blacks have any interest at all in trading their present white-created way of life for life in one of Africa's tribal societies.

"Nevertheless," some will say, "any world security program that must depend entirely on the far-sighted decency of most have-not nations might be too long a risk to take." Let's try "counting the votes" in a Bloc C as herein constituted. Here we come to one of the reasons for including in Bloc C such dictator-ruled white nations as Spain, Portugal, and Greece and such essentially nonwhite nations under white rule as those in Latin America and South Africa. Even though, by themselves, these might not total more than one third of the Bloc C votes, they and those wholly nonwhite nations that would with certainty always vote against any violation of the Unaforce charter would add up to well over one third. Thus the few nonwhite nations that could conceivably be "suckered" into throwing away their security by attempting to use Unaforce in a race war could never constitute the two thirds of all Bloc C nations necessary to control the Bloc C vote. And *without* the Bloc C vote, even a Peking which had miraculously gained control of the Bloc A vote would be helpless to promote any race wars.

Could a plurality of the "poor" nations in Bloc C successfully use the *threat* of supporting a Unaforce "takeover" by Bloc A, as a means to "bleed" the more prosperous nations of Bloc B? Such a bluff would have no plausibility because it would be obvious to all that if Bloc C thus encouraged a charter violation it would lose infinitely more in security than it could ever hope to gain financially by such a tactic.

THE *ALTERNATIVES* TO GIVING THE WORLD'S THIRD VOTE TO THE LEAST DEVELOPED NATIONS.

For those who have an uneasy feeling that even safer patterns than this one may be available for the voting control of a world enforcement agency, let us quickly review the well-worn alternatives:

A. Control by Veto of One Nation (as in U.N. Security Council) Is Undesirable.

Since most of the world's possible large-scale aggressors are members of the U.N. Security Council and since the veto of any one member can prevent the council from imposing any given penalty, any real enforcement of anti-aggression laws would be impossible under such a voting pattern, even if there were any clear-cut statutes in the U.N. charter to be enforced. The world has known for centuries that no police force can be trusted to make up its own laws as it goes along. Yet, by failing to incorporate in the U.N. charter a set of laws precisely defining what kinds of aggression are punishable, and precisely how they are to be punished, the creators of the U.N. charter made it necessary for its Security Council to perform a spur-of-the-moment legislative function before it could impose any penalty. Naturally, no major nation would have signed *that* kind of charter unless it *did* have veto power over any U.N. penalty action.

At the time the U.N. was founded, most of the nations felt temporarily *safe* about splitting hairs over the adoption of any basic anti-aggression laws because at that time good old, easygoing U.S.A. had a world monopoly of mass-destruction weapons; and nobody really feared the U.S. would use them unjustly. Each nation at the U.N. conference was "holding out for its pound of flesh" and thereby blocking adoption of any effective enforcement program. But today, the picture is very different. Now that some believe even an unreturned nuclear attack might wipe out a whole generation of babies; and now that Washington and Moscow realize that mere restraint on their part cannot insure the world against nuclear annihilation, much of the previous hairsplitting about national boundaries and definitions of aggression can probably be held to manageable proportions. The time is, at long last, right for getting the concessions necessary to the formulation of viable anti-aggression laws. However, the immediate point is simply that the voting pattern of the U.N. Security Council would make a Unaforce as impotent as the Security Council now is.

B. Voting Pattern of "General Assembly" Also Wholly Unsuitable for a Unaforce.

The danger of turning over invulnerable military power to any international agency controlled by such a voting pattern as that of the U.N. General Assembly is too obvious to need much discussion. If, instead of being divided among three Blocs, each representing different basic interests, the nations behind a Unaforce were all thrown into one big pot (as in the General Assembly), the plurality of "have-not" nations could use their invulnerable enforcement power to rob the "have" nations. Giving every nation in the world an equal voice in the voting may be fine for a mere debating society like the General Assembly, but a nuclear-armed Unaforce so controlled could never get the approval of the U.S., U.S.S.R., or the other more prosperous nations.

C. Equal Sharing of Control Between Free and Communist Nations Could Bring No Peace.

Even if the less powerful nations would agree to such a control pattern, any voting pattern that, in essence, shared the control of a Unaforce *equally* between the two groups of nuclear powers would be self-defeating. Allegedly "equal" partnerships usually result in an undercover struggle that ends in one partner being dominated by the other. Such a method of controlling Unaforce could only result in *perpetuating* the present world tensions. The major purpose of a Unaforce would be to solve those problems on which Blocs A and B cannot now agree. If control of Unaforce were evenly divided between the two groups now locked in a death-embrace, if there were no third vote to break the present deadlock, the world could only continue on toward Armageddon. A third vote on world enforcement problems is obviously an absolute essential for any lasting peace, and the safest place for that third vote is in the hands of those "weak" nations that would again become helpless pawns in the Great Power game if Unaforce were to violate its charter.

Anyone who thinks he has a sounder alternative for a Unaforce voting-control pattern than the one here proposed should lose no time getting it before the world.

WHY COMMUNIST BLOC A COULD NOT BE "DONE WRONG" BY BLOCS B AND C VOTING TOGETHER.

Even if Bloc B ever *wanted* to meddle in the internal affairs of

Communist nations, it could not possibly do so without getting Bloc C to nominate to the Unaforce staff men dedicated to violation of the charter. But, as previously demonstrated, there is every good reason to believe that at least two thirds of the Bloc C nations would never, under any circumstances, risk the wonderful new security Unaforce was giving them by voting for any charter violation.

As agreed to by all three Blocs at the time the charter was signed, Unaforce could and would solidly block any attempt at world conquest by Block A or any other Bloc. But in return for this concession on the part of the Communists, Moscow and Peking would get complete security from each *other,* as well as from the risk of a disastrous nuclear exchange with the U.S.

ANSWERS TO QUESTION 7 (JUST WHAT WOULD CONSTITUTE "PUNISHABLE AGGRESSION").

The types of aggression that Unaforce would be bound by its charter to punish in precisely prescribed ways would be spelled out in full by the original charter (and by possible later amendments if all *three* Blocs became convinced that more or better definitions were needed and feasible). It cannot of course be expected that any definitions concise enough and safe enough to be embodied in the charter could cover every conceivable petty annoyance that one nation might inflict on another. But reliable enforcement against the major kinds of aggression here defined could make the world an infinitely more secure and livable place than it now is—for *all* nations.

In order to define aggression soundly, without so many qualifying clauses as to make the definitions almost unreadable, we *first* need to provide in the charter rather precise classifications of (1) the various weapons that could be used in aggression, (2) the military potential and *degree* of threat posed by a given aggressor, and (3) the precise kinds of penalties to be imposed under specified conditions.

WEAPONS CLASSIFICATION TO BE EMBODIED IN CHARTER.

A. *"Weapons of Mass Destruction"*

This classification of weapons shall include all atomic, nuclear, and biological weapons, all chemical weapons (when used by one nation against another), and all other present or future weapons having *comparable "unit destructive power"* or comparable potential for *"massive surprise"* attack.

B. *"Other Military Weapons"*

This classification shall include all weapons having *less* unit-potential for destruction and *less* potential for "massive surprise" attack than Class A weapons, but having *more* destructive potential than Class C "normal police weapons."

C. *"Normal Police Weapons"*

Those weapons that, as normally used, injure only one person at a time. This category to include hand-guns, machine guns of less than 50 caliber, and weapons for the "non-injurious" control of small groups, such as tear-gas pistols, "water-cannon," and the like.

CHARTER CLASSIFICATION OF *NATIONS* (AS TO THEIR DEGREE OF POTENTIAL MILITARY THREAT TO UNAFORCE).

Class A Nations

Those known to possess substantial quantities of Class A weapons and/or facilities for producing same (presumably those nations under contract to produce such weapons for Unaforce).

Class B Nations

Those *not* suspected of possessing Class A weapons in quantity but having sufficient technological and industrial resources to create them in quantity.

Class C Nations

Those believed to have *neither* the resources to produce Class A weapons in quantity nor a stock of them on hand.

A FEW IDEAS FOR A GRADUATED SCALE OF *PENALTIES* TO BE EMBODIED IN CHARTER.

Penalty 1 (for minimal aggression by Class C nations)

Step A. When a nation responsible for one of the lesser categories of aggression has been fully identified by Unaforce direct observation, Unaforce radar, or decision of the World Emergency Court, it shall receive from Unaforce a formal warning. If within 72 hours thereafter the aggression has not ended, Unaforce shall issue a final warning. If the aggression has not ended within 48 hours after this final warning, Unaforce shall use Class B weapons to destroy what the Unaforce High Command estimates to be the necessary *minimum* of the aggressor's troop concentrations, military stores, and/or air force to end the aggression.

Step B. If such aggression then continues another 48 hours (without the aggressor's use of Class A weapons), Unaforce shall use Class B weapons to detroy *whatever* part of the aggressor's total military potential it finds necessary to quickly end the aggression. However, if the aggressor at any point, switches to the use of Class A weapons or attempts to counter-attack Unaforce, Unaforce shall be free to use immediately whatever minimum of Class A weapons its High Command finds necessary to end the aggression.

Step C. When such aggression has ended and the World Emergency Court has assessed the damage done and established a schedule of reparations payments by the aggressor, Unaforce shall use the minimum force necessary to insure payment of such reparations.

Penalty 2 (for aggression by Class B nations with Class B weapons)

Steps A, B, and C. Same as in penalty 1 above except that Unaforce shall give the fully identified aggressor nation only *one* formal warning and allow only 48 hours thereafter for all aggression to cease before imposing step A of the penalty.

Penalty 3 (for aggression by Class A nations starting with Class B weapons)

Step A. If the fully identified aggressor nation is continuing its aggression (without use of Class A weapons) 24 hours after receiving a *first* formal warning from Unaforce, Unaforce shall use Class B weapons to destroy the aggressor's capitol city as well as its major troop concentrations, military stores, and/or its most menacing air force and naval units.

Step B. If the aggressor (*without* resorting to Class A weapons), continues his aggression for another 24 hours or counterattacks Unaforce, Unaforce shall use whatever amount of destruction with Class B weapons it finds necessary to end the aggression. However, if at any point the aggressor switches to use of Class A weapons, or attempts to counter-attack Unaforce, then Unaforce shall be free to use *whatever* kind and amount of force its High Command finds necessary to end the aggression.

Step C. Same as step C of penalty 1.

Penalty 4 (for surprise attack with Class A weapons)

Step A. As soon as the identity of the nation responsible for the aggression has been fully established, Unaforce shall, *without* waiting to issue a formal warning, use Class A weapons (if it deems them absolutely necessary) to destroy whatever minimum of the aggressor nation's military potential it finds necessary to end the aggression without delay.

(Note here that although any large-scale use of Class A weapons by Unaforce might contaminate the atmosphere enough to endanger the whole world. Unaforce would not, in actual practice, ever *have* to use its Class A weapons—not so long as the potential attacker with Class A weapons knew beyond all doubt that Unaforce could and *must* impose this terrible penalty for such offense.)

Step C. Same as step C of penalty 1.

CATEGORIES OF *"PUNISHABLE AGGRESSION"* TO BE DEFINED BY UNAFORCE CHARTER.

Definition 1.

Use by any nation or its fully identifiable agent of any Class A weapon as herein defined to destroy life or property in another nation or in a Unaforce installation shall constitute the most severely punishable form of aggression and shall require Unaforce to impose on such aggressor, *without* warning, category 4 of the penalties herein prescribed, as soon as:

A. The source of such attack has been unmistakably identified by radar, satellite, or other Unaforce facility, or

B. As soon as the World Emergency Court has evaluated the evidence and determined that the missiles, submarines, bombers, satellites, secret agents, or other means of delivery of the attack were in fact under the control of the suspected nation.

(Note here that any *delay* of a few hours or even days necessary to obtain accurate identification of the nation responsible for such an attack with Class A weapons would not represent any serious *temptation* for that nation to attack. It would be fully aware of the invulnerability of Unaforce to any "first strike" with Class A weapons. And any "second strike" against Unaforce would be utterly impossible because, long *before* any nation could produce and install the vast array of Class A weapons necessary to give such a second strike even the remotest chance of success, that nation's aggressive intentions would have become obvious to the whole world. And any nation's buildup of such a huge illegal excess of Class A weapons would, in itself, be punishable under Definition 9 long before it reached a very dangerous stage. Also note that, under the Unaforce charter, the *detection* of any massively illegal buildup of Class A armaments, would be certain —without any worldwide "ground inspection" program—for reasons detailed in section H, under the heading "Other Provisions of the Charter."

Definition 2.

Any organized military attack with Class B weapons by one nation or its fully identified agents on the life or property of another nation or of Unaforce itself shall constitute punishable aggression. Such aggression shall require Unaforce to impose category 2 penalties if the aggressor is a Class C nation or category 3 penalties if the aggressor is a Class A or Class B nation.

Definition 3.

Use by one nation against another nation of Class C (police-type) weapons shall, when confirmed by the World Emergency Court, require that Unaforce proceed as prescribed by category 1 of the penalties herein provided.

Definition 4.

Any persistent *threats* by the government of one nation or its fully identified agents to use military force against another nation shall, when confirmed by a majority decision of the World Emergency Court, require Unaforce to impose category 1 penalties if the aggressor is a Class C nation or category 2 penalties if the aggressor is a Class A or Class B nation.

Definition 5.

The supplying of military weapons or of military manpower to a *revolutionary faction* of one nation by the government or fully identified agents of another nation shall (except as noted in the following text) constitute aggression punishable by category 1 penalties if the aggressor is a Class C nation or by category 2 penalties if the aggressor is a Class A or Class B nation. The *exception* to this definition of punishable aggression would be the possible case in which such military assistance to a revolu-

tionary faction of another nation had received the formal endorse-
ment of all *three* of the Bloc Administrative Commissions.

Definition 6.

Any physical force or threat of same used against the *person
or property or family of any member of the World Emergency
Court or of one of the Bloc Administrative Commissions* by the
fully identified agent of any nation shall constitute punishable
aggression. When the World Emergency Court has validated the
evidence of such aggression (by a majority decision), Unaforce
shall impose penalty 2 if the aggressor is a Class A or Class B
nation. If the aggressor is a Class C nation, category 1 penalties
shall be applied by Unaforce.

(Note here that any attempt to influence a Court Justice or
Bloc Commissioner by threats of mass destruction against the
nation he represents would be pointless because [unlike U.N.
representatives] each Justice of the World Emergency Court and
each member of a Bloc Commission would represent a plurality
of *all* the nations in the Voting Blocs. And even the maddest of
potential aggressors would not be silly enough to attack or
threaten a dozen or more nations at the same time.)

Definition 7.

Any private *individual* found guilty by a majority decision of
the World Emergency Court of using or threatening to use
physical force against the person or property or family of any
member of the Court or of a Bloc Commission shall be executed
by Unaforce, whether or not he can be identified as the agent of
some nation. And if such an individual was *not* provably acting
as an agent of some national government, the three persons
believed by the Court to be "nearest and dearest" to him shall be
executed with him. (Any feeling of revulsion against such a
ruthless penalty must be weighed against the fact that successful
threats against members of the Court or of a Bloc Commission
could jeopardize the lives of *millions* of at least equally innocent
people and against the fact that a madman undertaking such a

crime *without* encouragement from some government would not likely be deterred by fears for his *own* safety. Only the knowledge that his actions would cause the death of those nearest to him would be likely to deter such an "unattached" individual.)

Definition 8.

Any proven attempt to bribe a member of the Court or of a Bloc Commission or of Unaforce shall constitute aggression subject to the same penalties as under Definition 6 or 7, depending on whether such aggressor proves to be a national government or only a private individual.

Definition 9.

Any nation in which any Class A weapon is installed for test or use shall be considered a punishable aggressor, except where:

A. that nation is under contract to produce that weapon for Unaforce and has notified Unaforce one month in advance of its intention to install and/or test-use a specified number of such weapons at specified times and places, and

B. that nation has received from Unaforce written authorization to legally proceed with such tests.

Any nation accused by Unaforce of this category of aggression shall be given a 24-hour opportunity to *invite* Unaforce inspection of all its arms-production facilities. Failure by such a nation to issue such an invitation shall be considered important (though not conclusive) evidence of guilt.

If and when the World Emergency Court has established guilt under this definition, category 3 of the charter penalties shall be imposed by Unaforce.

Definition 10.

Installation in, or by, any nation of any device ruled by the World Emergency Court to be capable of *neutralizing* the effectiveness, in whole or in part, of any Unaforce weapon shall constitute aggression punishable by category 3 penalties, but only after the offending nation has received formal warning to destroy such devices and has failed to do so within 24 hours thereafter.

Definition 11.

Political propaganda as such shall *not* constitute aggression except when backed by use or threat of physical force. None of the above definitions of punishable aggression shall be construed to prohibit one nation from sending its propaganda agents into another nation, so long as they do not use or threaten the use of force. But neither shall any of these definitions be construed to prohibit any nation from forcibly *ejecting* from its territory the propaganda agents of another nation. And if such agents *refuse* to leave when ordered to do so, the nation ordering them out of its territory may imprison or execute them without committing aggression punishable by Unaforce. If, in such a case, the nation that sent its agents into another nation attempts to *retaliate* for their ejection, imprisonment, or execution with military force, such retaliation *shall* constitute aggression punishable by category 1 of the charter-prescribed penalties.

With these ground rules governing propaganda, any national government that cannot defend itself against its own revolutionaries probably would not deserve to survive. (For instance, Unaforce would have no power to prevent the people of South Vietnam from adopting a Communist government if its people could be talked into doing so *without* physical force or the threat thereof.)

Most of the enforcement problems which Unaforce might actually face in its first years would probably be due to the hot tempers of penny-ante dictators who, in a fit of rage, might *say* something which could be construed as a punishable threat. In such cases the prescribed penalties would probably never have to be imposed, because a formal decision by the Court that such an action or threat was punishable, together with a formal warning from Unaforce, would probably suffice to end such minor aggression. Likewise, those governments that, like naughty children testing the resolve of their parents, had an irresistible urge to test the firmness of Unaforce, might slyly edge a toe over the legal line until they were fully satisfied that Unaforce was not just another toothless U.N. Compliance by national governments with international law (like compliance of children with parental edicts) will be influenced more by the absolute *inevitability* of punishment than by the severity of the initial penalty.

ANSWERS TO QUESTIONS 8 AND 9 (WHAT KIND OF *"WORLD EMERGENCY COURT"* WOULD BE NEEDED?).

As spelled out on a preceding page, the U.N.'s "International Court of Justice" would be wholly unfitted to adjudicate the actual enforcement of world anti-aggression laws. Also, the kind of world court needed in the "Unaforce age" would, to some extent, be affected by the fact that, with a militarily invulnerable Unaforce in operation, attempted aggression would be certain to take some entirely *new forms*. Even an "unbalanced" dictator, for instance, would not be stupid enough to launch nuclear missiles from his own territory—not when Unaforce radar could reliably determine the trajectory and source of such an attack and thereby make his nation immediately subject to inescapable annihilation. On the other hand, if some nations's capitol city were suddenly wiped out by Class A weapons *smuggled* in by some other nation's agents, Unaforce could not be empowered to punish the suspected nation until the evidence had been fully assessed by an experienced judiciary having the same type of "political balance" as Unaforce itself. Or if Israel, for instance, should accuse Egypt of threatening a military attack (or vice-versa), a judicial decision on the evidence would be needed from a court, a plurality of whose members would always reflect the interests of Voting Blocs *other* than that of the aggressor nation.

The evidence to be weighed by a World Emergency Court would have to be "dug up" by someone. Neither Unaforce nor the World Emergency Court, as here envisioned, would have any worldwide secret service of its own. Instead, as elsewhere detailed, each Bloc Administrative Commission would need, and have, a worldwide "investigative staff" of its own. Also, the secret services of the individual nations in each of the two Voting Blocs *not* in sympathy with the aggressor nation would be able and anxious to help identify the source of any major aggression. Unaforce officials would themselves have daily access to the premises of any company producing weapons under a Unaforce contract. In addition, (since no nation can long prosper without extensive world trade), any massive arms buildup by any nation would doubtless be detected and reported to Unaforce by commercial travelers, newsmen, or airline pilots long before it could reach a very dangerous stage. All in all, the gathering of reliable *evidence* of punishable aggression should be no problem nor take very long.

A "World Emergency Court" would then need to be covered by some charter provisions such as the following:

A. *Composition of Court and Method of Election.*

It should perhaps have 15 Justices—five from each of the three Voting Blocs and not more than one Justice from any one nation. These justices should be elected (and if necessary, quickly impeached) by the process elsewhere outlined for the election of Bloc Administrative Commissioners. However, unlike the Bloc Commissioners, the Justices would be elected (by a plurality of the "Heads of State" in that Bloc) *for life*—up to the mandatory retirement age of 70.

Since one third of the 15 Court members would have been elected by (and would therefore reflect the composite viewpoint of) a plurality of the Heads of State in each of the Voting Blocs, it seems safe to assume that two thirds of the Court (like two thirds of the Blocs that elected them) could always be depended on to oppose any aggressor's attempt to violate the charter.

B. *Headquarters for the Court.*

The number and diversity of the cases to come before this specialized anti-aggression court would probably be only a fraction of the case-load carried by an ordinary court—at least after the Court's first year or so of operation. For this reason such a special World Emergency Court might have to be in session only a total of a few weeks out of a given year. It might be feasible for it to hold each of its brief sessions in a *different* nation of its own choice, thereby insuring that it would never find itself in session in a nation that it was "trying" for aggression. Such a "floating" court might also further minimize the risk of external pressures, since it would always have the added protection of the *local* police in a nation of its own choice. Such a plan would also permit each Justice to make his home where his family *wanted* to live, instead of having to spend the rest of their lives in some one "foreign" city like Geneva or the Hague. Travel allowances for Court members should be ample for each Justice to take his family along on at least some of these short trips. Such a set-up (including top compensation) should help to make the world's foremost jurists available for this Court.

C. Exhaustive screening, top pay, and unparalleled prestige to minimize risk of corruption of Justices.

The actual screening of each Bloc's candidates for the Court would be in the hands of the three Bloc Administrative Commissions whose worldwide investigative staffs would be in *competition* with each other to expose any phase of a candidate's character, training, and past performance that might fall below the exceedingly stiff standards embodied in the charter.

Like the Unaforce High Command and the Bloc Administrative Commissioners, the Justices of the World Emergency Court obviously should be among the world's highest-paid public servants. Even so, they would represent a great cash *saving* for the nations of the world, compared to the cost of the world's present military outlays. Because these Justices would be among the world's best paid and most honored men they would be very difficult to corrupt, even if any attempt to corrupt them were *not* subject to the terrible penalties provided by the charter.

D. Special safeguard against "natural" bias by a Court Justice.

Any member of the Court whose homeland was involved (as an accused or accuser) in a case before the Court would of course be disqualified for service on that particular session of the Court. Since not more than one Justice could be from a single nation, that disqualification would normally reduce the number of "active" Justices in a particular case to 14 or 13—without disturbing to any serious extent the Court's original "political balance." Remember that the three Voting Blocs are so constituted that a *plurality* of the nations in each of two of the Blocs could always be depended on to oppose any aggression that would violate the charter. And since all of the Justices from those two Blocs would represent the viewpoint of the plurality of *nations* in those two Blocs, it is safe to assume that at least 10 of the 15 members of the Court could also be depended on to oppose any given violation of the charter. Assuming that *all* of the four remaining Justices from the aggressor's Bloc might be biased in favor of the aggressor, the nine remaining Justices (from the two Blocs opposed to the violation) would *still* constitute more than a plurality of all the Justices sitting on that particular case.

E. Why This Court Could Not Be Successfully Threatened by an Aggressor.

No would-be aggressor would dare to try to influence a given court decision by *threatening* a member of the court because any such threat would in itself constitute aggression punishable by a militarily invulnerable Unaforce. Since the only reason anyone would *want* to threaten a member of this court would be to keep him from voting to penalize a nation or individual *already* accused or suspected of aggression, the chance that such threatener might escape detection and terrible punishment would be far too slim a chance to tempt anyone. Even if the entire court were captured and held hostage by an aggressor nation, that would not in the least prevent Unaforce from imposing the charter penalty for such aggression. Unaforce would have no choice.

ANSWERS TO QUESTION 10 (WHY WOULD "BLOC ADMINISTRATIVE COMMISSIONS" BE NEEDED? HOW SAFEGUARDED?).

Because very little latitude for personal decisions could be allowed to the staff in direct control of Unaforce weapons, and because the World Emergency Court could not be burdened with such matters as the investigation and selection of nominees to the Unaforce staff, each of the three Voting Blocs would need its *own* "Bloc Administrative Commission."

Each of these three 9-member Bloc Commissions (with its own undercover investigative staff) would have responsibilities as follows:

1. Investigation, evaluation, *and* nomination to the Unaforce staff of that Bloc's one third of all Unaforce recruits below the level of the High Command. (Nominees would be subject to final appointment or rejection by the High Command of Unaforce.)

2. Investigation and evaluation, *only,* of seasoned Unaforce officers whom that Bloc Commission considered suitable for nomination to positions in the High Command. (Actual nomination of such officers would be by the assembled Heads of State in *each* Bloc. Final election of each such High Command officer would be by two of the three "Bloc Votes," which would properly reflect the world's *balance* of interests.)

3. Each Bloc Commission would have the privilege (not the duty) of investigating a nominee of either of the *other* two Bloc Commissions to make sure he measured up to the stiff charter specifications for that job. The findings of any such "cross-investigation" would be made available for the consideration of the assembled "Heads of State" who would elect.

4. Each Bloc Commission's undercover staff would investigate for its own "Heads of State" all candidates proposed to those Heads of State by their own "Judicial Committee" for

that Bloc's one third of the 15 Justices on the World Emergency Court.

5. Each Bloc Commission would be required to assist the Unaforce High Command and/or the World Emergency Court in accurately identifying (and tracing the affiliations of) any accused aggressor or threatener whose identity could not be quickly and fully established by Unaforce itself.

6. Any two of the three Bloc Commissions would have the power to effect quick *preliminary* impeachment (and temporary removal from duty) of any member of the Unaforce High Command or of the World Emergency Court. *Final* impeachment or reinstatement would be by the Heads of State "voting by Bloc."

7. Any two of the three Bloc Commissions would have the power to *veto* the release of a given "major" purchase contract by Unaforce. The charter would spell out what constitutes a "major" contract.

8. The three Bloc Commissions (voting by Bloc) might even serve as a "Court of Last Resort" for low-level Unaforce personnel who had been court-martialed by their own officers. In the ordinary army, where the court-martial process is usually *not* subject to civilian review, there could be a small possibility that a handful of insurgent officers might be able to cow some of their subordinates by a threat of secret court martial into aiding them in a subversive conspiracy. The suggested review procedure could insure against that hazard in Unaforce. (If the World Emergency Court, which would be less familiar with the daily flow of Unaforce operations, were to be burdened with the detail of these "minor" appeals cases, it might be less instantly available for its more crucial responsibilities.)

In the light of their awe-inspiring responsibilities, the members of each Bloc Commission would need to be elected by a process safeguarded at least as well as that governing the choice of the Unaforce High Command. Each of the nine Bloc Commissioners for a given Bloc would (after the first nine years of Unaforce operation) be elected for a nine-year term. But only one would be elected each year, so that a given Bloc Commission would always consist of 8 experienced members and only one new one. Each year, then, each nation in a given Bloc would be privileged to *nominate* one candidate for Bloc Commissioner. If one of the less influential nations in the Bloc felt that one of its own nationals would have little chance of election, that nation would also have the privilege of merely endorsing the nominee of some other nation in that Bloc.

In any case, each nation putting forward a nominee for Bloc commissioner would have thoroughly investigated him in relation to the charter specifications covering his integrity, intelligence level, emotional stability, education, past performance and so on. But in addition (6 months before the annual election date), each nominating nation would have supplied to the Heads of State of all other nations in that Bloc with a complete transcript of its nominee's life record, so that each of the other nations in the Bloc could, if they wished, "cross-investigate" the nominee.

The annual voting procedure of the Heads of State (assembled within their own Bloc) could cope effectively with the large number of nominees involved, because all of the electors (each a Head of State or his fully empowered designate) would be assembled in the same room and could readily keep calling the roll until the "weaker" nominees were eliminated and two thirds of the electors could agree on the same candidate.

The members of each Bloc Commission would themselves elect their own Chairman, again by a two-thirds vote.

Protection of Bloc Commissioners From Illegal Attempts To Influence Their Decisions. A would-be aggressor nation would not dare try to influence (by bribes or bodily harm or threat of force) the decision of these Bloc Commissions. Such aggressor nation would know in advance, beyond all doubt, that the militarily invulnerable Unaforce would have no option but to impose terrible penalties for any such attempt. The chance that the secret services of the Bloc Commissions themselves (plus the secret services of powerful individual nations) might not be able to identify accurately the nation *behind* any such attempt would be far too slim a chance to be tempting. Furthermore, each Bloc Commissioner (like each member of the World Emergency

Court) would always have the kind of secret-service "shield"
from *individual* madmen that leading Heads of State are now
given.

ANSWERS TO QUESTION 11 (SOME OF THE *OTHER*
PROVISIONS NEEDED IN CHARTER).

*A. Provision to Help Insure That Each "Bloc's" Single Vote
Would Always Reflect the Will of the PLURALITY of All
Nations in That Bloc.*

Within any one "nation" (where the voting is done by millions of people scattered over a wide area), the cost of a whole
series of *successive* ballots for the same office would be prohibi-
tive.
The whole voting population would have to be recalled to the
polling booths many weeks in succession. For this reason, most
"national" elections must be finally decided by one or two ballots
per voter, with the result that such elections can result in the
election of a candidate wanted by only a minority.

By contrast, under the Unaforce charter it would be feasible
to require that each Voting Bloc's decisions or candidates would
all represent the composite will of at least a plurality of all the
Heads of State in that Bloc. This would be entirely practical
because none of the Voting Blocs would have more than 80 or
so Heads of State, all of whom (or their fully empowered designates) could be assembled once a year in the same room. And if
their first (or fifth or tenth) ballot failed to result in a two-thirds
victory for some one candidate or policy, they would (at no great
extra expense) *continue* balloting until a plurality of their votes
did coincide. Thus election of the Unaforce High Command and
of the Emergency Court Justices and of the Bloc's Administrative
Commissioners would be safeguarded in a way and to a degree
not possible when an official is elected by "popular vote."

In those typical cases where no two of the three *original* Bloc
votes were for the same candidate or policy, the Heads of State
(or their fully empowered delegates) of all *three* Blocs would
remain in session until two of the Blocs *did* come to agreement
on the same candidate or policy. In short, the proceeding would

be something like that of an American "party convention"—
except that none of the electors would be mere party hacks. They
would all be sovereign Heads of State (or their fully empowered
designates).

The annual sessions of each Bloc's Heads of State would
be held within that Bloc's *own* territory. Since these Heads of
State would *not* be meeting to vote the imposition of penalities
but only to elect certain officials, such events would hardly tempt
any would-be aggressor to risk harming or threatening such
group, not when such aggressor would thereby put himself at the
mercy of a military invulnerable Unaforce that had an inescapable obligation to impose intolerable penalties for such aggression.

B. A Charter Provision Would Eliminate Vacillation As an "Invitation" To Aggression.

No matter how heavily armed a nation like the U.S. or the
U.S.S.R. may ever be, its government, before actually using any
mass weapons, must always stop to consider the consequences to
its great cities and industries. Because such a government *does*
have an option to use or not use its weapons in a particular
situation, some other nation is eventually sure to think it may be
able to "run a successful bluff." And eventually *that is certain to
lead to world disaster*. But a Unaforce (which would have no
tempting targets of its own to be attacked with mass weapons)
would not *need* to stop and consider consequences. Nor would
it be *privileged* to vacillate. When any nation had been fully
identified as a violator of the Unaforce charter, that charter
would give Unaforce no option but to carry out the penalties
prescribed by the charter. The whole success of a Unaforce operation would hinge on the absolute inevitability of prescribed
punishment for specified offenses, as soon as such offenses had
been fully verified. Knowing this, no nation would be "tempted
to test" Unaforce as it might be tempted to test another national
government. Under Unaforce there would be no more of the
insidious blackmail of nations that now keeps the world teetering
on the brink of irretrievable disaster.

*C. A Charter Provision Would Ensure the Communists One
Man in the Unaforce High Command.*

Even though one third of the total Unaforce *staff* would be
nominated by Communist Bloc A, the U.S.S.R. would doubtless
balk at any Unaforce program that did not also guarantee to
Bloc A that one of the three members of the Unaforce *High
Command* would always be from Bloc A. Considering that, in
many matters, Bloc A not only could be, but almost surely would
be, outvoted by the other two Blocs, such a provision would be
only fair. Since Blocs B and C would have no *reason* to vote
against Bloc A except to prevent some potential violation of the
charter, the interests of Bloc A could not be seriously jeopar-
dized anyway. But Blocs B and C (if the charter did not provide
otherwise) probably would pool their voting strength to elect *all*
the Unaforce High Command from their own two Blocs. That,
of course, would be unacceptable. So the charter would provide
that *NONE* of the three Voting Blocs would ever be without at
least one man on the Unaforce High Command.

D. Charter Provisions to Safeguard Investigative Procedures.

As discussed in a previous paragraph, certain aspects of any
truly secure world-peace enforcement program would (unhap-
pily) require the services of *competing* undercover investigative
staffs, each representing not the interests of any one nation but
the *composite* interest of the plurality of all the nations in one
given Bloc. Each of these three "Bloc Investigative Staffs" should
probably be under the immediate supervision of its Bloc Administrative Commission. But as part of the overall Unaforce system
of "checks and balances" each such Investigative Staff should
probably have the "privilege of appeal" direct to the Heads of
State in its Bloc—just in case its findings ever indicated that the
decisions of its Bloc Commission were seriously in conflict with
the best interests of the plurality of nations in its Bloc.

The charter should also closely define the permissible purpose
and scope of investigation by these staffs, limiting their activities
to such fields as:

1. Searching out and confirming the personal history, character, and personality, of possible *nominees* to the staff of Unaforce, the World Emergency Court, and a Bloc Commission.

2. *Identifying* beyond doubt the nation or individual responsible for what the charter defines as a "punishable aggression."

3. Investigating charges of *conspiracy* to commit punishable aggression.

4. Gathering of *evidence* regarding a member of Unaforce, a Bloc Commission, or the World Emergency Court who had been accused of violating (or conspiring to violate) his oath of office.

The charter should further provide that although any nation would have the right to order any identified Bloc Investigator out of its territory and the right to imprison him if he was caught thereafter, his uninvited presence would *not* constitute "punishable aggression" by any of the nations of the Bloc he served. In short, these Bloc undercover men, like all other international spies throughout history, would understand when appointed that they would be largely "on their own" as regards their personal safety if detected.

ANSWERS TO QUESTION 12 (WHEN AN UNDER-
DEVELOPED NATION NEEDS TEMPORARY AID IN
GOVERNING ITSELF, HOW WOULD IT BE
PROTECTED FROM EXPLOITATION?).

Unaforce's responsibility in such a situation would be merely to give the vulnerable nation complete and permanent security from takeover by any stronger nation, except in a case where all *three* of the Voting Blocs agreed that most of the people of the weaker *nation* actually wanted to merge with a stronger nation for their lasting economic advantage. But for at least several decades to come, truly voluntary mergers between nations would be rare. The more immediate need would be for a mechanism to replace "imperialism" as an interim stabilizing factor for the weakest of nations during their "incubation period." Many such nations cannot yet govern themselves wisely in the computer age simply because not enough of their people have yet had the training and experience they need. But they can't quickly *get* the needed training, experience, and modern tools without huge donations or long-term loans from more advanced and prosperous nations. The more advanced nations are getting very tired of pouring their hard-earned surplus into incompetently governed and graft-ridden nations, only to see their gifts or loans thrown away on grandiose prestige schemes or on ludicrously miscalculated "giant steps." How then, can this vicious circle be broken *without* the traditional takeover by some empire-builder?

In the days when primitive peoples were usually taken over and ruled by more efficient and stronger nations, such takeovers seldom resulted in adequate training of the native people for real self-government. But such a takeover by an empire-builder did at least provide substantial "stability" in the lives of the conquered people—a stability very sorely missed by the people of some of today's ex-colonies. Even today's *rulers* of some of the illiterate and underdeveloped nations are doubtless very aware that a mere infusion of "pump-priming" funds cannot produce important gains for their people unless someone with more know-how than they themselves have can temporarily impose a degree of discipline and organization on their confused people. But at present, such rulers of their people don't *dare* invite a temporary "caretaker" government from outside because they know any such "temporary" caretaker might turn out to be a permanent exploiter.

Moscow and Peking have been more than eager to fill the aching void left by the voluntary dissolution of the British, French, and other empires. But the idea of exchanging British or French masters for Russian or Chinese masters naturally has no appeal to the people who need *temporary* supervisory help. How then can both financial and administrative aid to under-developed nations be permanently *divorced* from exploitation of such helpless nations?

With a bluff-proof Unaforce in operation (to insure that an interim government supplied to such a nation would remain "interim" and not develop into a permanent tyranny) and with a permanent international pool of top-caliber technicians and administrators (under the supervision of the Joint Bloc Administrative Commission), this ancient vicious circle *can* be broken. It would then be feasible to limit the availability of huge aid funds (from the World Bank), to those needy nations that would agree in advance that all *disbursals* of such funds would be under the control of competent and experienced officials appointed and controlled by the Joint Bloc Administrative Commission. Unsound performance by such internationally appointed disbursement officers could, of course, be appealed by the borrowing nation to the Commission itself. By controlling the purse-strings on a sound new program of mass education, such international disbursement officers could probably get whatever authority they needed to supplement the local police system with temporary help from an international pool, so that lack of law and order would not jeopardize the investment and wreck the program. But only when such disbursement officers are appointed and controlled by an agency that is itself safeguarded from domination by aggression-minded nations, can they be trusted by the beneficiary nation. Because no arm of the U.N. *is* so safeguarded, no U.N.-appointed supervisory officials could be fully trusted by a nation in need of temporary supervisory help. But appointees of the Joint Bloc Administrative Commission here envisioned could be trusted, because the control of that Commission would always be in the hands of the two Blocs opposed to aggression by any nation.

The integrity of the U.S.-appointed "Governor-Generals" who conscientiously readied the Phillipine people for self-government should give other needy and largely illiterate nations confidence in an aid program temporarily administered by foreign officials, if that program were under the right *kind* of international agency.

One reason why the control of such monetary and supervisory aid to underdeveloped nations cannot be entrusted to the U.N. is that the creditor nations (in Blocs A and B) could not afford to have their funds disbursed at the whim of the debtor nations that control the U.N. General Assembly. Also, since the

U.N. cannot safely be given invulnerable police power, it would often be hopelessly handicapped in any effort to aid governments like those in the Congo and Nigeria that must integrate warring factions before making any kind of progress. Only something like the Unaforce and the Joint Bloc Administrative Commission here proposed could be trusted by needy nations to give them unselfish as well as competent supervisory assistance, on a truly interim basis.

ANSWERS TO QUESTION 13 (FINANCING OF UNAFORCE COSTS).

For the present, of course, a disproportionate share of the cost of setting up and operating the Unaforce program would have to be borne by the two Great Power Blocs (A and B). But even if just the U.S. and the U.S.S.R. were to divide the total cost between them for the first few years, the saving to these two nations compared to their *present* total military costs would be an important one. However, since most of the American and Russian "weapons in being" could safely be turned over to Unaforce (and would probably be all that Unaforce would need for several years), the many other prosperous nations, could be expected to finance needed island real-estate, uniforms, food, and salaries from the start.

As time goes by, most of the Bloc C nations (with assured world peace and really *constructive* aid programs) will also become prosperous and able to bear an increasing share of Unaforce costs. The Unaforce charter should contain a *flexible* formula for distributing Unaforce costs—perhaps one based on a small percentage of each nation's annual governmental budget. But the cost obviously could never be allocated arbitrarily by thirds against each of the three Voting Blocs.

With each nation assessed strictly in proportion to its real "ability to pay," and with Unaforce on the job to enforce collection, there would be no more of the past nonsense about "uncollectable" dues. When the World Emergency Court had found invalid a nation's excuses for failure to pay its relatively modest Unaforce dues, the Court would so notify the delinquent; and if that nation still failed to meet its responsibilities, Unaforce would impose on such a nation an initial penalty even milder than any of those already proposed but which should be enough to get prompt action from such a debtor nation.

ANSWERS TO QUESTION 14 (WHY ALL NATIONS WOULD BE AT LEAST AS SAFE FROM A PERVERSION OF UNAFORCE POWER AS THE U.S. WAS SAFE FROM ITS OWN MILITARY ESTABLISHMENT WHEN THAT ESTABLISHMENT HAD A WORLD MONOPOLY OF ATOMIC WEAPONS).

Remember that the only way Unaforce could seriously harm any nation would be by actually *violating* its charter, because its charter would specifically forbid it to interfere in the domestic affairs of any nation (except as specifically authorized by the charter and approved by all *three* Voting Blocs). Unaforce would be far less likely to violate its charter than the U.S. government might be to violate its Constitution because:

A. Extremely Limited Scope of Unaforce Duties and Authority Would Help Make Unaforce Less Vulnerable to Subversion than the U.S. Government Is.

Whereas U.S. military men and their families would nearly all suffer acute *personal* hardship if the U.S. were grossly misgoverned and whereas, in such a case, they might be susceptible to revolutionary or subversive appeals, no amount of misgovernment by the world's individual nations could be blamed on Unaforce and used by a demagogue to brainwash and subvert Unaforce personnel. Unaforce would have no responsibility for the misgovernment of any nation. Anyone trying to persuade Unaforce men to violate their charter would have to do it *without* the one tool which has always proved most effective for that purpose—the tool on which Lenin, Hitler, and Castro chiefly relied. Unaforce personnel then, could be persuaded to violate their charter *only* by bribery, blackmail, mistaken loyalty to a homeland bent on aggression, or by appeals to hurt pride and power-madness. Let's examine, one at a time, these possible roads to subversion of Unaforce:

1. *Bribery.* Whereas some U.S. military men can perhaps be bribed without too much difficulty because they may feel underpaid or feel their profession is not adequately honored or because they are simply weak or vicious characters, the world could afford to pay even the lowest rank of Unaforce officer enough to support his family in luxury *without* taking bribes. And the knowledge on the part of all Unaforce men that they were the most thoroughly investigated and carefully chosen large body of men in the world would create an unparalleled *esprit de corps* among them. The congenitally weak or vicious men who are readily bribed in the ordinary national army simply could not get appointed to the Unaforce staff in any numbers.

2. *Blackmail.* Whereas the huge army of any major nation like the U.S. normally finds it necessary to accept a lot of men having "blackmailable" weaknesses that can be used by enemy agents to subvert them, the life record of every nominee to the small Unaforce staff would be so exhaustively screened by competing secret services that a would-be aggressor could find very little "blackmailable" material among them.

3. *Loyalty to an Aggression-Bent Homeland.* In the U.S. military establishment (or the Russian or the Chinese), any type of appeal that could induce even a few "decent" men to violate their oath "for the glory of our homeland" would likely also be effective with most of the others. But even those Unaforce men from the same Voting Bloc would be from many different homelands, each with its own very different set of problems and attitudes. Trying to subvert any high proportion of Unaforce personnel with an appeal to their "local patriotism" would be vastly more difficult than a similar attempt would be in the U.S. (or other strictly national) army.

4. *Appeals to Hurt Pride or to Power-Madness.* No big national army can afford to screen its inductees intensively enough to eliminate even most of those who were born power-mad neurotics or who, in their youth, suffered the kind of

humiliation which turns some boys into potential power-grabbers. But the world *can* afford such tight screening for all Unaforce candidates, and would get it, because three different Bloc Commission Investigative Staffs would be *competing* to uncover such cases. But suppose some of these more rigidly screened Unaforce men became embittered by some fancied humiliation *after* they joined Unaforce? Here again, no mere national army could *afford* to promptly retire *on pension* every officer whose performance necessitated demotion but did not warrant court-martial. Nor could a national army afford to pension off every high-level officer who had to be by-passed year after year in the awarding of promotions. But the world could well afford to do just that as regards key officers of Unaforce—to thoroughly insulate them from possible demagogic appeals to "hurt pride."

B. Comparative Loss of Invulnerability.

If the U.S. military establishment, when *it* had a world monopoly of Class A weaons, had used its invulnerable military power to set up a military dictatorship in the U.S., it would *not* immediately have lost its invulnerability to successful attack because there were no comparable weapons in the hands of anyone else in the world. But if Unaforce should betray its trust and try to set up a world dictatorship of its own, it would *instantly* lose its invulnerability because it would then be claiming huge cities and industries that would become prime targets for every outraged smuggler of Class A weapons. If Unaforce were taken over by some aggressor *nation,* that nation could then be held hostage to immobilize the seized Unaforce.

C. U.S. Military Men Cannot Protect Their Families from Mass Annihilation by Merely Honoring Their Oath of Office, But Unaforce Men Could Do So.

The family of a U.S. soldier *has* no security from mass annihilation. But Unaforce men *would* have such protection for their families, as long and *only* as long as Unaforce adhered strictly to its charter.

D. U.S. Could Have an Administration Elected by a Dangerous Minority, But Only a Plurality (of the Three Bloc Votes) Could Elect a Unaforce Administration.

In the U.S., even 35% of the popular vote could elect a President and a Vice President under certain circumstances. And if such a minority President were dizzy enough to use the military force at his command in violation of the Constitution, he could conceivably set up a military dictatorship before he could be stopped. Or he could gradually weaken the U.S. defense posture enough to leave the U.S. at the mercy of foreign enemies.

By contrast, the pattern here presented for the election of the top Unaforce officials insures that no minority, or even a simple majority, could ever control the election of the top Unaforce officials. This Unaforce pattern is made feasible by the fact that a total of only three votes would be cast for each of these top Unaforce officials—one by each of the world's three Voting Blocs. And each of the three Bloc Votes would, in turn, always represent the collective will of a *plurality* of all the Heads of State in that Bloc. This difference between the U.S. and the Unaforce voting patterns would be an important factor in making Unaforce *less* vulnerable to subversion than the U.S. government is.

E. The U.S. Could Have Taken over World Control Without Violating Its Own Constitution. Unaforce Could Not Do So.

When it had a worldwide monopoly of Class A weapons, the U.S. could easily have set up its own world dictatorship *without* violating its own Constitution. But Unaforce could not do so except by grossly violating its charter and as already noted there are many good reasons why Unaforce would be less apt to violate its charter than the U.S. is to violate its constitution.

So, for above many reasons, a Unaforce staff could be made *less* vulnerable to subversion than was even the U.S. military establishment of the late 1940s.

ANSWERS TO QUESTION 15 (WHY THE IDEAS WHICH
MAKE THIS UNAFORCE PLAN WORTH INTENSIVE
STUDY BY THE WORLD'S BEST MINDS HAVE NOT
BEEN PUBLISHED BEFORE NOW).

In 1946, by the time the author (then a wartime federal
official) was able to complete the first crude draft of this Unaforce pattern, the "timing" for its publication had become
impossibly bad. The U.N. had just been launched with great fan-
fare and obviously could not be sidetracked at once for an entirely
different program, no matter how much greater a long-term
potential such a new program might have. Publication of this
document just then might only have lessened whatever faint
chance the U.N. ever had of maintaining world peace.

And even at the time that first draft was completed it was
apparent to the author that any *immediate* publication would
be premature— that the America of the late 1940s was in no
mood to consider any program for a lasting world peace that involved even the tiniest sacrifice of its "glorious sovereignty."
Those were the years when the U.S. had a world monopoly of
atomic weapons and was short-sighted enough to bet its whole
future that it could 'jawbone" the rest of the world into acting
sensibly for generations to come. Publication of these ideas would
have been futile so long as the U.S. was on that "invincibility
jag."

But then a funny thing happened on the way to Armageddon.
Some of the prominent Americans who had been allowed to
examine THE original draft of this material apparently passed
along some of its ideas to writer-friends who thought them too
good to be buried even temporarily. These writers devised
emasculated versions of this basic program calculated to have
some immediate appeal to even the absurdly cocky America of
the early 1950s. In doing so, they of course *omitted* those devices
most essential to the proper performance of such a mechanism
and most needed to prevent its subversion. But even these relatively impotent and therefore "painless" prescriptions for an

effective peace-keeping mechanism failed to ripple the blind complacency of the nation in the early fifties.

Then, during the *late* fifties and the sixties (from the time the Kremlin became a nuclear power until the Red Chinese recently began to threaten Moscow in a big way), publication of this Unaforce plan would have met only with derision because, during those years, the Russians were taking *their* turn at imagining themselves invincible. Like the America of the late forties, the U.S.S.R of the late fifties and the sixties was in no mood to cooperate on any plan for a lasting peace that involved relinquishing one iota of national sovereignty. But right now, for a short time, the situation is different. Right now, before Red China is finally ready for its nuclear showdown with Moscow, the timing is *exactly right* for dissemination of a program that makes solid sense, based on the cold facts of human nature.

Whether the creation of a militarily invulnerable World Anti-Aggression Enforcement Agency *precedes or follows* a war costing many hundreds of millions of lives, the eventual adoption of such a pattern seems inevitable. There is simply no alternative except everlasting exposure to sudden mass annihilation. If we now *wait* until Peking considers itself ready for a nuclear showdown with Moscow, the remnants of the human race will curse us for our blindness and inertia.